MW00604745

THE

RUMFORD

COMPLETE

COOK BOOK

BY

LILY HAXWORTH WALLACE

GOLD MEDALIST

GRADUATE OF NATIONAL TRAINING SCHOOL OF COOKERY
LONDON, ENG.

PRICE, ONE DOLLAR

PUBLISHED BY THE

RUMFORD CHEMICAL WORKS

PROVIDENCE, R.I.

V-41

Teo 7489.08

HARVARD COLLEGE LIBRARY
BEQUEST OF
MRS. CHESTER N. GREENOUGH
SEPTEMBER 20, 1926

Copyright, 1908,
By The Rumford Chemical Works,
Providence, R.I.

641.5
W19

Printed by
The University Press, Cambridge, Mass., U. S. A.

This scarce antiquarian book is included in our special *Legacy Reprint Series*. In the interest of creating a more extensive selection of rare historical book reprints, we have chosen to reproduce this title even though it may possibly have occasional imperfections such as missing and blurred pages, missing text, poor pictures, markings, dark backgrounds and other reproduction issues beyond our control. Because this work is culturally important, we have made it available as a part of our commitment to protecting, preserving and promoting the world's literature. Thank you for your understanding.

PREFACE

THE recipes in this book have been carefully tested, and if measurements and general instructions are followed, the result in every case will be satisfactory.

The author has endeavored to give clear and concise instructions for the best dishes of their kind; rather than take up space for repetition of the same general recipe varied only in flavoring, form of baking and other minor detail.

It will be noted in the table of weights and measures that all measurements are given as LEVEL. Unless otherwise stated in the individual recipe, this rule should always be followed.

Ideas vary as to what constitutes a rounding or heaping spoon or cupful, while LEVEL is or should be the same the world over — as much as spoon or cup will hold, then leveled off with a knife.

It is not claimed that these recipes are all new. Some are original; some the gift of friends who have experimented till good results were obtained; some are old family recipes, never before printed; while others are standard rules that have stood the test of years and are still at the head of their respective lists. However, all have been tested and may be used by the novice with the same certainty of success as when the ingredients are combined by the experienced cook.

LILY HAXWORTH WALLACE.

WEIGHTS AND MEASURES

1 cupful	= ½ pint.
4 cupfuls	= 1 quart.
3 teaspoonfuls	= 1 tablespoonful.
1 gill	= ½ cupful.
16 tablespoonfuls of liquid	= 1 cupful.
2 cups butter packed solid	= 1 pound.
4 cups sifted flour . . .	= 1 pound.
9 large eggs	= 1 pound.
2 cups granulated sugar .	= 1 pound.
2 tablespoonfuls butter .	= 1 ounce.
4 wineglassfuls	= 1 cupful.
4 tablespoonfuls	= 1 wineglassful.
60 drops	= 1 teaspoonful.
4 tablespoons flour . . .	= 1 ounce.

Teaspoonfuls and tablespoonfuls are measured level unless otherwise stated.

One-half spoonful is measured lengthwise of the spoon.

Cupfuls are measured level full.

A set of measures (quart, pint and half-pint) should be in every kitchen. The graduated measures divided into quarters, halves and thirds are best. A graduated glass measure is also advisable for the correct measurement of liquids.

A set of accurate scales is also indispensable to good cooking and housekeeping.

TABLE OF CONTENTS

(vii)

How to Avoid Objectionable Baking Powders

READ THE LABEL

EVERY baking powder should show on the label in plain language all its ingredients, so that the public may know whether it contains *alum* or other unhealthful material. The Pure Food laws generally require this.

Scientific names are sometimes used on the labels of alum powders, such as "sulphate of alumina," "aluminum sulphate," "sodium aluminum sulphate," etc., instead of the plain word *alum*, but whenever the word alumina or aluminum appears it means some form of *alum*.

Some alum baking powders contain a little ordinary phosphate and are then called "phosphate," or "alum-phosphate" baking powders; but of course the addition of the phosphate does not remove the unhealthful alum quality.

All baking powders which contain alum, by whatever name they may be called, or whatever other ingredients they may contain, should be avoided.

Rumford Baking Powder does not contain alum in any form, but is a strictly pure phosphate powder in which is used the latest improvement of the genuine Professor Horsford's phosphate made by us solely for our own preparations, and none of which is ever sold for use in other baking powders.

DEFINITIONS OF TERMS

USED IN COOKERY

A la Creole. Cooked with tomatoes, onions and peppers.

A la Printanière. A soup or stew served with young spring vegetables.

Aspic. A savory jelly for meats, fish, vegetables and salads. Frequently used as a garnish.

Au Gratin. Cooked with browned crumbs and usually with grated cheese.

Bain-marie. A vessel containing hot water in which other vessels containing foods are placed to keep hot without further cooking. Literally a double boiler on a large scale.

Bechamel. A rich white sauce made with stock, milk or cream.

Bisque. A thick white sauce or soup generally made from shellfish.

Blanch. To whiten by scalding.

Bouillon. A meat broth.

Bombe. Moulded ices having the outside one variety and the centre another.

Bouquet of Herbs. A bunch of various flavoring herbs, used for soups or stews.

Braise. To cook in a closely covered stewpan with vegetables, having a gentle heat, that neither flavor nor juices are lost by evaporation.

Canapé. A finger strip of bread or toast spread with a savory compound, usually either fish or egg, daintily garnished and served as an appetizer before lunch or dinner.

Croustades. Small pieces of bread fried or toasted. Used as a garnish for minced or hashed meat.

En Brochette. Small portions of meat, such as chicken livers, cooked with bacon on a skewer.

Entrée. A savory made dish served as a course itself, or between heavier courses, at dinner.

Farci. Stuffed.

Fondue. Cheese and eggs cooked together.

Frappé. Half frozen.

Glacé. Glazed over. In savory dishes with meat-stock, boiled down to a glaze; in sweet cookery, iced or brushed over with white of egg.

Hors-d'œuvres. Small dishes served during the first course of a dinner.

Jardinière. Mixed vegetables.

Lard. To insert strips of fat pork or bacon in meats deficient in fat, with a larding needle.

Macédoine. A mixture of vegetables or fruits.

Marinate. To make savory in a mixture of seasonings: oil and vinegar, or oil and lemon juice.

Meringue. White of egg and sugar beaten together.

Mousse. May be savory or sweet. A light, frothy mixture thickened with gelatine, whipped with a whisk till spongy in texture and then packed in ice and salt for three or four hours.

Mulligatawny. A rich soup flavored with curry.

Pâté. A small pastry shell, usually made from puff paste. May contain either a sweet or savory filling.

Purée. Meats, vegetables, fish, etc., cooked in liquid till tender, then passed through a sieve.

Roux.   A cooked mixture of butter and flour for thickening soups, sauces and gravies.

Salmi.   A rich stew of game, half roasted and then cut up and cooked in a sauce.

Sauté.   To cook till brown in a shallow pan with a little fat.

Soufflé.   Puffed up and made light by use of well-beaten eggs.   May be savory or sweet.

Vol-au-vent.   A very light case of puff paste in which savories or sweets may be served.

RUMFORD
" The Wholesome "
Baking Powder

Pure and Wholesome. Rumford is different from and superior to all other powders. It is made of the genuine Professor Horsford's phosphate (prepared especially and solely for this purpose), which has been commended by the most eminent physicians for its wholesomeness. The phosphates are natural components of meat and grains, and are food elements necessary for the maintenance of health. They are essential constituents of the human body, and a deficiency results in loss of strength and consequent health. Fine wheat flour is deprived of phosphates in the bolting process, and is, therefore, lacking in this invigorating quality. Rumford Baking Powder adds these strengthening phosphates to the food.

Perfect Baking Quality. The action of Rumford Baking Powder in the dough is thorough, making cake, biscuit, muffins, etc. of finer texture and flavor, and which will retain their fresh condition longer, than if made with ordinary baking powder or cream tartar.

No Baking-Powder Taste. Rumford contains no alum or cream of tartar, and imparts no bitter or baking-powder taste to the food. It will not impair the most delicate flavoring used in cake, puddings, etc. Biscuit made with Rumford not only possess the natural flavor of the grain, but can be eaten hot without the discomfort which so often follows when they are made with yeast.

Reasonable Price. By a specially improved process of manufacture we are enabled to sell Rumford at a cost much less than the ordinary high-priced baking powders.

OUR GUARANTEE UNDER THE PURE FOOD LAW IS ON FILE WITH THE SECRETARY OF AGRICULTURE, WASHINGTON, D.C., No. 221.

The Rumford Complete Cook Book

SOUPS

SOUP STOCK

TO each quart of cold water allow one pound meat and bone in about equal proportions; one pint of cleaned vegetables, such as carrot, onion, celery, etc., cut in pieces; one bunch soup herbs, being a sprig of parsley, two bay leaves, and any dry herbs of which the flavor is desired, such as thyme, summer savory and marjoram; seasoning of salt and pepper to taste, together with a little celery seed or celery salt if fresh celery is not in season.

Wipe the meat and cut into small pieces that it may more readily give off its juices; chop the bones and put them with the meat in the stock-pot; then add the vegetables and soup herbs. Pour the water, which must be cold,* over them and bring very slowly to the boiling point; skim if necessary and cook slowly for six hours, keeping the stock-pot closely covered. The stock must then be strained and left uncovered in a cool place till cold, that the fat may be more easily removed. The bones, meat and vegetables are sometimes cooked a second time with more water to make what is known as "second stock," not so strong as the first, but better than water for thick soups, sauces and gravies.

If a highly flavored and colored stock is wanted, the vegetables and meat are sometimes browned in a little fat before the water is added, but this is not advisable where a clear stock is desired. Beef is the

---

*Cold water draws the juices out of the meat into the liquid. Boiling water hardens the outside of the meat and prevents the juices being given off.

1

meat most commonly used for brown stock, and veal or chicken with a little ham for white stock. Cooked meats and the trimmings from steaks and roasts may be added to the other ingredients in the stock-pot, but have not the same food value as fresh meats.

Stock should never be left to cool in the stock-pot, but always removed to a clean, cold vessel and left uncovered in a cool place till wanted for use.

All marrow should be removed from the bones before cooking. It can be used to better advantage in other ways.

For family use where fair sized joints are frequent, it should be rarely necessary to buy meat for soups, the bones and trimmings furnishing enough, with a judicious use of vegetables and flavorings, for ordinary use. The same rules, previously given, apply to the making of stock under these conditions if a little less water in proportion to the meat is used.

Ox-tail Soup

2 tablespoons drippings or lard.	2 stalks celery.
2 ox-tails.	2 quarts cold water or stock.
1 large onion.	2 tablespoons pearl barley.
1 carrot.	1 tablespoon flour.
2 sprigs parsley.	2 tablespoons cold water.
1 bay leaf.	¼ cup sherry.
	Salt and pepper, or cayenne.

Melt the fat and fry in it the carrot and onion cut into dice, also the ox-tails which have been cut in pieces. When brown add the water, also the celery, parsley and bay leaf tied together. When boiling put in the barley and simmer four hours. Remove the large bones, celery, parsley and bay leaf, and thicken the soup with the flour rubbed smooth with two tablespoons of cold water. Season rather highly, add the sherry, and serve.

Mutton Broth

2 pounds neck of mutton.
2 quarts cold water.
1 level teaspoon salt.
1 small turnip.
1 small carrot.

1 small onion.
2 tablespoons barley.
1 teaspoon chopped parsley.
Extra salt, and pepper to taste.

Wipe the meat, cut it into small pieces and place in a saucepan with the cold water; let it come slowly to the boiling point and then add the salt, which causes any scum there may be to rise. Simmer for an hour, skimming occasionally. Add the vegetables cut into dice, also the barley, and cook till the vegetables are quite tender; season to taste. Add the chopped parsley just before serving.

Turkey Soup

1 turkey carcass.
Water to cover.
1 small onion.

1 stick of celery.
½ teaspoon extract of beef.
2 tablespoons rice.

Seasoning to taste.

Break the carcass in pieces and remove all the stuffing; add water to just cover, and simmer two hours with the celery and onion; then remove the bones, strain, and add the extract of beef, and then the rice which should have been previously cooked in boiling salted water. Let the soup reach boiling point, season and serve with croutons of fried bread.

Tomato Bisque

6 fresh tomatoes or one can tomatoes.
1 small onion.
1 bay leaf.
2 cloves.
1 sprig of parsley.
2 tablespoons butter.

2 tablespoons flour.
1 pint milk.
½ teaspoon baking soda.
1 teaspoon hot water.
Salt and pepper to taste.
1½ pints water if fresh tomatoes are used.

Cut the tomatoes in slices and stew them till tender with the onion, bay leaf, cloves, parsley and water. If canned tomatoes are used omit the water.

When tender pass all through a sieve, rubbing the pulp through also. Blend the butter and flour in a saucepan till smooth, but not browned; add the hot tomato and stir till boiling. Season, and after cooking five minutes put in the soda dissolved in a teaspoonful of hot water. The addition of the soda neutralizes the acid of the tomato. Just before serving, add the milk previously scalded.

Cream of Oyster Soup

1 pint oysters.
1 quart milk.
1 tablespoon butter.

1 tablespoon flour.
Salt and pepper to taste.
1 cup whipped cream.

Chop the oysters, drain off the liquor and add to it an equal amount of water; heat slowly, skim well, then put in the chopped oysters and cook three minutes. Scald the milk, thicken with the butter and flour creamed together and add to the oysters with the seasoning. Put in the cream the last moment before serving.

Clam Chowder

1½ dozen clams chopped fine.
1 cup water.
3 large potatoes cut into dice.
2 slices pork or bacon cut into dice.

1 sliced onion.
1 quart milk.
2 tablespoons butter.
2 tablespoons flour.
1 teaspoon chopped parsley.
1 teaspoon salt.
⅛ teaspoon pepper.
8 crackers.

Heat the pork or bacon and fry the onion in the fat; add the clam liquor, water and potatoes; cook until tender, season, and add the clams and milk. Cook ten minutes longer, then thicken with the butter and flour creamed together. Pour the chowder over the crackers and sprinkle with the chopped parsley.

Clear Soup

1 quart stock.	A few slices of vegetables
¼ pound very lean beef.	similar to those used in
Whites and shells of 2 eggs.	the stock.

Seasoning and garnish.

Mince the meat finely, add the whites of the eggs, slightly beaten, also the shells, and mix with half a pint of the stock. When well blended, add with the vegetables to the remainder of the stock; whisk while heating, then when hot leave it over the fire without touching till it boils. Cook very gently five minutes longer; add half a cup of cold water, and after it has stood ten minutes strain through a fine cloth that has been wrung out of hot water and spread over a bowl or attached to a soup stand. If the first liquor which runs through the cloth is not quite clear pass it through again.

Remove any grease that may be on top of the soup by passing small pieces of blotting or tissue paper over it, so as to absorb the globules of fat; then season with salt, celery salt, cayenne, and lemon juice if the flavor is desired. Color, if necessary, with caramel (the soup should be the color of sherry), and serve plain or with any of the following garnishes:

GARNISHES FOR CLEAR SOUPS

FOR JULIENNE SOUP: To each quart of clear soup add one-third cup each carrots and turnips, cut into strips an inch long and about the thickness of a match, and boiled in water till tender.

FOR BRUNOISE SOUP: To each quart of clear soup add two-thirds cup of mixed vegetables cut into one-fourth inch cubes, or cut into fancy shapes with a vegetable cutter, and boiled in water till tender.

FOR MACARONI SOUP: To each quart of clear soup add half a cup of macaroni cooked in boiling salted water till tender, and cut into rings.

FOR CONSOMMÉ ROYAL: Make a custard, allowing two tablespoons of milk to each egg used. Beat the egg and milk together and season to taste; strain the custard into a cup, and either place the cup in a saucepan of water over the fire and cook till the custard is set, or place the cup containing the custard in a vessel of water in the oven and cook till set. In either case, as soon as the custard is set, cut it into dice with a knife, or into any fancy forms for which you have cutters, and drop into the soup just as it is served.

SOUP CROUTONS

Cut stale bread, without crust, into half-inch cubes and fry golden brown in hot fat. Or cut slices of buttered bread into cubes and crisp in a hot oven. Either drop into the soup just before serving or hand with it.

MEMORANDA

MEMORANDA

FISH

TO BAKE FISH

HAVE the fish well washed, and if it is haddock, small cod or any small whole fish, the black skin on the inside can be removed by rubbing briskly with a cloth or small brush dipped in salt. Dry the fish and, if to be stuffed, prepare the stuffing by the rule given below; place it in the fish and sew up the opening with white thread. Lay the fish — either flat or fastened with thread or skewers in the form of the letter S — in a well-greased baking-pan, preferably one kept for this purpose, dredge with flour and put a little dripping or bacon fat over the top. If the oven is very hot cover the fish with a greased paper during the first part of the baking to prevent its becoming too brown. Baste frequently with the fat that is in the pan, adding more if needed. Unless the fish is well basted it is likely to be dry. Serve with a sauce or gravy.

Stuffing for Baked Fish

3 slices stale bread.
2 tablespoons chopped suet.
1 small onion, finely minced.
1 tablespoon chopped parsley.
Salt and pepper to taste.
1 small egg, and a little milk if needed.

Soak the bread in cold water till quite soft, mash it till smooth and add to it the suet, onion, parsley, seasonings and egg. Moisten, if necessary, with a little milk — the mixture must be just firm enough to keep its shape — and fill the fish, sewing up the opening as soon as the stuffing is in place. This same mixture may be rolled into small balls, baked in the pan with the fish, and served as a garnish if preferred.

9

TO BOIL FISH

Choose a small, compact fish or a firm slice of a large one. Wash thoroughly and wrap in cheese cloth, tying the ends of the cloth loosely. If a regulation fish kettle with drainer is used, it will be easier to remove the fish from the pan after cooking; or a plate may be placed in the pan and the fish laid on it. This prevents any possibility of the cloth sticking to the bottom of the pan and also makes it easier to remove the fish when cooked. A tablespoon of vinegar in the water will keep the fish a good color and make the flesh firmer.

The water should be quite hot, but not boiling, when the fish is put in. If plunged into actively boiling water the skin is likely to crack. To prevent this still further the water should only simmer during the time of cooking. The average time allowed for the cooking of boiled fish is about six minutes to the pound, unless very thick, when ten minutes should be given. When small fish are boiled whole the heads are always left on, but the eyes removed.

The fish usually boiled are cod, haddock, halibut, mackerel and salmon.

TO SAUTÉ FISH

Clean the fish thoroughly, wipe dry and dip in either flour, egg and bread crumbs, or egg and corn meal, and sauté in a shallow frying-pan, having only a little fat in the pan. Cook till one side of the fish is brown, then turn with a fish turner, or a thin, flexible knife, and brown the other side. The fish may be seasoned either before or after cooking. The fat used may be either lard, butter, drippings, oil, or bacon fat. Small fish, such as pan-fish, porgies, flounders, butterfish, or slices of larger fish — halibut or cod — are suitable for this method of cooking.

TO FRY FISH

Clean the fish and wipe perfectly dry; then dip in beaten egg and afterwards in bread crumbs or corn meal, but preferably in the crumbs, patting these on well that no loose ones may fall off and burn in the fat; then plunge the fish, a few pieces at a time, in the fat which must be smoking hot and of which there must be sufficient in the pan to completely cover the fish. Cook golden brown, and drain well before serving.

For full directions as to the preparation and heating of the fat, see instructions for Frying, page 29.

TO BROIL FISH

Wipe well, season with salt and pepper, and place between the wires of a well-greased broiler. Broil the flesh side first, then the skin side, turning often during the cooking process.

The more oily fish, such as bluefish, salmon, herring and mackerel, are best for broiling, though other kinds are often cooked this way. When the drier varieties are broiled they must be well seasoned after cooking, and butter spread and lemon juice sprinkled over them just before serving.

Baked Bluefish in Perfection

1 large bluefish.	Salt, pepper and a little
⅓ cup melted butter.	onion juice.
Juice of half a lemon.	

Split the fish down the back, wipe it well and lay in a greased baking-pan. Melt the butter and add to it the salt, pepper, onion and lemon juice, and pour a little of the mixture over the fish. Place in a hot oven and bake about half an hour, basting with the prepared butter every ten minutes. Serve very hot with or without a sauce.

Perfect Fish Balls

2 cups raw potatoes.   1 tablespoon butter.
1 cup flaked codfish.   ⅛ teaspoon pepper.
                1 egg.

Cut the potatoes in small pieces and cook with the
fish till the potatoes are tender. Mash very thoroughly till every lump is gone; add the butter, pepper and egg, and beat again till the whole is light
and creamy. Take up a little of the mixture at a
time with a spoon that has been dipped in hot fat
— this prevents the mixture sticking to the spoon —
and drop into a pan containing plenty of smoking-
hot fat. Cook golden brown — if the fat is the
right heat this will not take more than a minute —
drain well and serve with or without bacon.

Fish Timbales

2 cups raw cod, haddock   2 eggs.
    or halibut.   Seasoning of salt, pepper,
1 cup bread crumbs.   lemon juice and Worces-
½ cup cream.   tershire sauce.

Chop, mince or grind the fish till quite fine; add
the crumbs, cream and seasoning. Beat the whites
and yolks of the eggs separately, the whites to a
froth and the yolks until thick. Add the yolks first
and mix them well in; then just before cooking, fold
in the whites, mixing only enough to blend them
with the other ingredients. Turn into well-greased
moulds — plain ones are best, as the contents are
likely to turn out better — and steam half an hour,
either in a saucepan over the fire, or in a covered
pan containing boiling water, in the oven. In either
case let the water come halfway up the sides of the
moulds and keep the pan closely covered. Serve on
individual dishes with a sauce poured over them.

Codfish Fritters

Strips of salt codfish.	1 egg.
2 tablespoons flour.	⅓ cup milk.
¼ teaspoon salt.	Frying fat.

Cut the fish into strips about the size of the finger and soak over night. In the morning drain and dry. Make a batter by putting the flour into a bowl with the salt, adding the yolk of egg and the milk, and beat well to remove all lumps. Beat the white of the egg to a stiff froth, add to the batter and dip the strips of fish into it, one at a time. Drop at once into hot fat, having enough fat in the pan to completely cover the fritters; cook golden brown and drain well before serving.

Scalloped Oysters

1 quart oysters.	1½ cups cream and milk
2 tablespoons butter.	mixed.
2 tablespoons flour.	½ cup buttered crumbs.
Salt and pepper to taste.	

Put the butter and flour together into a saucepan and cook till the butter is melted and blended with the flour; add the cream and milk, a little at a time, and cook till the mixture boils. Cook five minutes longer and then add the seasoning.

Grease a baking-dish and put a little of the sauce in the bottom; cover with oysters which have been carefully examined and all bits of shell removed. Add more sauce and more oysters till the supply is exhausted, having sauce for the top layer. Cover with the buttered crumbs and bake about twenty minutes in a hot oven. Serve as soon as done that the oysters may not become tough.

To Prepare the Crumbs. Melt one tablespoon of butter in a frying-pan or saucepan and, when hot, add the crumbs to it, stirring till they have absorbed the butter. By this method the butter is equally distributed instead of being in little patches, some of the crumbs greasy and others dry.

This method may be used for scalloped fish.

Fried Oysters

2 dozen oysters.	Fine bread crumbs.
2 eggs.	Seasoning.

Wipe each oyster dry and sprinkle with salt. Beat the eggs just enough to mix yolks and whites, and dip in the oysters so as to coat all parts with the egg. Lift them gently and let any excess of egg drip away; then drop each oyster into the crumbs, which should be spread on a paper or plate — preferably the former, as they will be easier to handle. When coated with crumbs, shake gently to remove any that may be loose, and set aside till all are done. Fry golden brown in smoking-hot fat.

Always use bread crumbs for frying in preference to cracker crumbs. The latter absorb grease, while the bread crumbs throw it off.

TO BOIL LOBSTER

Put a handful of salt into a kettle of boiling water, into which place the lobster head first. Boil from twenty to thirty minutes, according to size. Too long or too rapid boiling will make the meat tough and stringy.

In buying a lobster choose one that is heavy for its size; very large ones are likely to be tough. The male lobster is best for boiling, but the female is preferred for salads and sauces on account of the coral.

To prepare the coral for use, remove it from the lobster and place on a tin in a moderately hot oven till quite dry, but not discolored; then pound in a mortar and sift. This will keep and is valuable as a garnish for salad and for use in sauce.

TO BROIL LOBSTER

Take a live lobster and split down the back, beginning at the head, and remove the stomach and intestines. Open fully and place on a broiler, cook the flesh side first, then the shell side; crack the large claws, and serve very hot with melted butter, lemon and Chili sauce.

Lobster Croquettes

The meat of one good-sized ½ cup milk.
  lobster (boiled). A grating of nutmeg.
1 tablespoon butter. Salt and pepper to taste.
1 tablespoon flour. 1 teaspoon lemon juice.
  Egg and bread crumbs.

Mince the lobster meat as finely as possible, adding the coral if there is any. Cream the butter and flour in a saucepan and, when mixed, add the milk, and cook to a stiff sauce; add the salt, pepper, lemon and nutmeg, and mix well. While still hot add the lobster and spread on a plate to cool, having the mixture about half an inch thick. When cold, shape into cutlet form, using the blade of a flexible knife and the fingers, or roll with the hands into the shape of very thick corks, or form with the hands or a tin mould into cones; dip in egg and bread crumbs as directed for the frying of fish (page 30), and fry golden brown in smoking-hot fat. Drain well before serving.

Stuffed Fillets of Fish

2 tablespoons butter. Lemon juice.
2 tablespoons flour. Seasoning to taste.
¾ cup milk or fish stock. 8 fillets of fish.
½ cup chopped shrimps, lobster or mushrooms.

Melt the butter and blend the flour with it; pour in the milk slowly, stir until boiling, season and add the mushrooms or shrimp. Trim the fillets of fish neatly, spread with the mixture, fold and fasten with a small skewer. Bake in a moderate oven, covering the pan with greased paper, and adding one-half cup of water to prevent burning. Serve with horseradish sauce.

Shrimp Patties

1 cup picked shrimps, either fresh or canned.	1 egg yolk.
1 cup cream sauce.	1 teaspoon lemon juice.
	Salt and pepper to taste.

Slight grating of nutmeg.

Make the sauce by beating together in a saucepan two tablespoons butter with the same quantity flour; then stir in half a cup thin cream and the same of milk. Stir until boiling, cook five minutes, put in the seasonings, and the shrimps which may be divided if very large. Heat thoroughly and, just before serving, add the yolk of the egg. Fill little puff paste cases and serve.

Moulded Fish

1 cup cold minced fish.	1 cup white sauce.
2 eggs.	1 tablespoon parsley.

First make the sauce by blending two tablespoons butter with the same quantity flour then stir in slowly one cup milk or cream, and cook three minutes after the sauce boils. Season to taste with salt, pepper and lemon juice; add the parsley, fish and yolks of eggs. Beat the whites of the eggs to a stiff froth and fold them in. Half fill small moulds with the mixture, and bake or steam half an hour. Serve with horseradish sauce.

MEMORANDA

MEMORANDA

MEATS

THE CHOICE OF MEATS

IN considering how to buy meat, we must look at the relative cost as compared with the nutriment to be gained from the different cuts no less than at the qualities which go to make good meat. The most expensive portions of the animal are not necessarily the best, for more nutriment can be often obtained from a cheaper cut, provided proper care and time are taken for the cooking. Much unnecessary expense is incurred in housekeeping, because meals are not planned sufficiently in advance to allow the cheaper cuts, which require long cooking, to be used.

The meat of young animals is more tender but less nutritious than that from animals of mature growth.

Beef and mutton — the standard meats — are always in season; but lamb is at its best in the summer and fall, veal in the spring and early summer, while pork should be eaten only in the colder months.

The best beef is the flesh of a steer about four years old. It should be bright red in color, firm, and marbled in appearance from the blending of fat and lean which shows even feeding and that the animal has not been rapidly fattened for killing. There should be also a fair proportion of creamy white fat next the surface.

Lamb and mutton have a larger proportion of fat than beef, and the fat is harder. Good mutton is thick, the flesh fine grained and of a bright color. The strong mutton flavor, so often found, can be practically eliminated by the careful removal of the pink skin above the fat on the outer surface of the meat.

Lamb is smaller and lighter in color than mutton. One distinguishing test between the two is that in lamb when the bone is broken or cut, as in the case of a leg or chops, it will be found red and rough;

19

while as the animal grows older the blood recedes from the bones and leaves them white and smooth.

The flesh of veal should be pink and the fat white. If the flesh is white it denotes that either the animal was too young or was bled before killing. In either case when the flesh is white it is better avoided.

Veal must be very thoroughly cooked; is difficult of digestion and contains less nutriment than beef, mutton or lamb. It is somewhat tasteless and requires more seasoning than other meats.

Pork is another of the less wholesome meats. While obtainable during all seasons, it should be eaten only in winter, and then sparingly. Pork contains a larger proportion of fat than any other meat and requires long, slow cooking. The fat should be a clear white and the lean pink. Salt pork, bacon and ham are more wholesome than the fresh meat; and bacon fat is considered by physicians to be a more valuable and easily assimilated form of fat than any other.

All meats should be removed from the wrapping papers as soon as received, wiped with a damp cloth and placed near, but not directly on, the ice.

The processes most commonly employed for the cooking of meats are, roasting, broiling, stewing and boiling.

TO ROAST MEAT

First, wipe with a damp cloth, then skewer and tie if necessary to keep the meat in shape. For beef, mutton and lamb allow fifteen minutes for each pound and fifteen minutes over; for veal and pork twenty minutes to the pound and twenty minutes over. These close-grained meats are very indigestible unless well cooked. Some cooks flour meat before roasting.

As the object in roasting is to keep the juices within the meat it is necessary to apply intense heat at first, so as to sear the outside and form a firm coating through which the juices can not escape. Therefore, when roasting, have the oven sufficiently hot when the meat goes in to accomplish this result. At the end of fifteen minutes the heat may be reduced and the cooking proceed more slowly. The meat should be frequently basted with the fat that flows from it, to prevent the outside becoming burned or dry. It may also be dredged or sprinkled once or twice with flour and salt. Some cooks use covered roasting pans, claiming that the meat is kept more moist and the work of basting eliminated.

TO BROIL MEAT

Broiling is practically the same method as roasting, but is applied to smaller pieces of meat, only choice portions being suitable for this method of cooking. The fire must be hot and clear, the object being, as in roasting, to keep the juices in the meat and, therefore, it is necessary to sear the outside quickly. When this is done the meat should be moved a little farther from the fire and the cooking proceed more slowly. The broiler should be slightly greased and heated before the meat is placed on it. When broiling by gas have the burners lighted fully seven minutes before the meat is placed under them, that the heat may be sufficient to sear the outer surface at once; otherwise the meat is likely to be tough and dry.

TO STEW MEAT

In stewing, the less expensive parts of meat are utilized and, consequently, plenty of time must be allowed for the cooking. If hurried, toughness is almost inevitable. By this method of cooking some of the juices are drawn out into the gravy. Meat may be stewed by itself or with the addition of various vegetables; it may be also enriched by frying both meat and vegetables in a little fat before adding water or stock, both color and flavor being improved if this is done. It is a decided advantage, when possible, to prepare a stew the day before it is to be served, as the fat can be removed from the gravy more easily when cold. Stews made from meat which has been cooked once will naturally require more seasoning and flavoring with sauces and other condiments than when fresh meat is used.

A stew is better and more savory if the gravy is browned, seasoned and thickened before the meat is added.

TO BOIL FRESH MEATS

In boiling, it is intended that the greater part of the juices shall be retained in the meat. Therefore place the joint, after wiping, in boiling water and keep it boiling about five minutes, with the object of hardening the surface and preventing the goodness being drawn out into the liquid. Twenty minutes to the pound and twenty minutes additional should be the time allowed.

The water must be boiling (212 degrees) when the cooking begins, but 135 degrees (simmering heat) will suffice after a few minutes. Far more food is spoiled by the application of too much heat than too little. Very gentle bubbling will indicate the right temperature of the water.

Meat is sometimes steamed by cooking in a closely covered steamer over boiling water. By this method there is very little weight and practically no goodness lost, but a longer time — thirty minutes to the pound — must be allowed.

In boiling salt meats, the method is changed, as they are put into cold water that the slow heating may draw out some of the salt. In the event of the meat being more than ordinarily salt, the first water is sometimes thrown away when it reaches boiling point, and fresh added.

The liquor in which fresh meat has been boiled makes a good foundation for soup stock. That from salt meat, if not too salt, may be utilized for bean or pea soup.

Broiled Lamb

Slices of cold roast or boiled lamb.

2 tablespoons olive oil.
1 tablespoon lemon juice.

Salt and pepper.

Cut the slices of meat about half an inch thick from a part of the joint that is not too well cooked. Mix the oil and lemon juice together and let the meat stand in the mixture for an hour. The oil will enrich, and the lemon make the fibre of the meat tender. Place the slices in a broiler and cook about four minutes over a hot fire. Season rather highly, and serve with currant jelly or maître d'hôtel sauce.

Hot-Pot

2 pounds of lamb suitable for stewing.
2 pounds potatoes.

4 onions.
Salt, pepper and a little flour.
Water or stock.

Cut the meat into pieces convenient for serving. Peel the potatoes and cut them into small, thick pieces; slice the onions thinly. Mix the salt, pepper and flour and roll each piece of meat in the mixture. Put a layer of potatoes in a deep dish or bowl (a wide-mouthed bean pot is a satisfactory dish), then a layer of meat, next sliced onion, repeating the process till the dish is filled. Have potatoes for the last layer and fill the dish with water or stock. Bake three hours in a moderate oven, adding more water if necessary. Serve in the dish in which it is cooked.

Brown Stew of Lamb

2 pounds of lamb.
2 onions.
2 carrots.
1 head celery or a little celery seed.

2 tablespoons drippings.
1½ tablespoons flour.
1½ pints water or stock.
Salt and pepper.

Cut the meat into pieces convenient for serving. Peel the onions, scrape the carrots and wash and scrape the celery.

Melt the drippings in a saucepan and fry the meat golden brown on all sides, removing as soon as browned; put in the flour and brown that also. Add the stock or water and stir till boiling; then put in

the meat and the prepared vegetables. Season to
taste, and cook very slowly for two hours.

Irish Stew

2 pounds mutton suitable   6 small onions.
  for stewing.   1 small carrot.
8 medium-sized potatoes.   Salt and pepper.
      About 1½ pints water.

Cut the meat into pieces of convenient size for
serving. Remove some of the fat and put the meat
into a saucepan with the water which should be
almost at the boiling point; add the onions peeled
and cut into thin slices, also the carrot scraped and
sliced. Cook very gently — the water should only
simmer, for hard boiling would toughen the meat —
and at the end of an hour add the potatoes, peeled
and cut in thick pieces. Season to taste with salt
and pepper, and continue to cook till the potatoes
are tender. Then serve all together on one dish.

Stuffed Shoulder of Mutton

1 good-sized shoulder of   Grated rind of half a lemon.
  mutton.   1 tablespoon chopped suet
1 cup bread crumbs.   or drippings.
1 tablespoon chopped pars- Salt and pepper to taste.
  ley.   1 egg.

Remove the blade bone from the shoulder, or have
the butcher do it. Put the bread crumbs into a
bowl with the parsley, lemon, suet, salt and pepper,
and mix them with the egg well beaten. Stuff the
cavity from which the bone was removed, sew up
the opening, and roast, basting frequently with a
little fat or the meat will be dry.

Allow fifteen minutes to the pound. Serve with
a thick, brown gravy. Other dressings may be used
if preferred.

Beefsteak Pie

1½ pounds round steak.   ⅓ teaspoon pepper.
1 tablespoon flour.   Plain paste.
1 teaspoon salt.   Cold water.

Cut the meat in thin slices, and a little fat into very small pieces. Mix the flour, salt and pepper on a plate, and dip each piece of meat into it. Place a little fat in each piece of meat and roll up. Lay these rolls of meat in a pie dish, and fill the dish about two-thirds with cold water. Cover the dish and bake in a moderate oven for one and one-half hours. When the meat is tender, cover with a plain crust, the rule for which is given under "Pastry," and bake half an hour longer.

Pot Roast of Beef

4 pounds top sirloin of beef.	Seasoning.
	Onions, carrots and turnips.
2 tablespoons flour.	3 tablespoons drippings or
1 quart water.	other fat.

Have the meat cut in a thick, compact piece. If necessary, tie and skewer so that it will keep its shape.

Melt a little fat in a saucepan (an old-fashioned, round bottom "Scotch bowl" is the best), and brown the meat on all sides; pour the boiling water over it and cover closely. Simmer as gently as possible for two hours; then season, and add the vegetables scraped or peeled as they need, and cut into pieces. Cook till the vegetables are tender; then remove the meat and vegetables from the pan and thicken the gravy with the flour mixed smoothly with a little cold water. If necessary add more water while the roast is cooking that there may be sufficient gravy to cover the vegetables.

Cannelon of Beef

2 pounds round steak.	2 tablespoons chopped pars-
2 tablespoons bread	ley.
crumbs.	1 small chopped onion.
Grated rind of half a	2 tablespoons melted butter.
lemon.	1 egg.
Salt and pepper to taste.	

Chop the meat finely, or run it through a meat chopper; add the bread crumbs, lemon rind, onion, parsley, butter, seasoning and beaten egg. Mix well and form into a long roll; lay on a greased tin and cover with greased paper. Bake three-quarters of an hour, basting every ten minutes with a little hot water and melted butter or drippings.

Turn onto a hot dish and serve with gravy or mushroom sauce.

Beef Olives

1½ pounds very thin round steak.	1 slice of onion, minced.
⅓ cup rice.	2 tablespoons beef drippings.
1 tablespoon chopped parsley.	2 tablespoons flour.
	Salt and pepper to taste.
A pinch of sweet herbs.	½ cup stoned olives.
	1 pint water or stock.

Cut the meat into pieces about four inches square. Chop the trimmings and add to the rice, parsley, herbs, onion and seasonings to form a stuffing. Put a spoonful of this mixture on each slice of meat, roll up and tie firmly. Heat the drippings and cook the rolls in them till brown; then remove from the pan, add the flour, mix smoothly and put in the water or stock, whichever is being used. Stir till boiling, replace the meat and cook very gently one and one-half hours. Five minutes before serving add the olives. Remove the strings from the meat before dishing.

Veal Cutlets

1½ pounds veal cutlet cut thick.	1 small egg.
	Bread crumbs.
Seasoning.	

The meat may be either cut into pieces or left whole, as preferred. Season with salt and pepper and dip each piece into well-beaten egg; drain and drop onto a paper of bread crumbs; coat thoroughly and shake off all loose crumbs. Melt and heat a little fat in a frying-pan, and cook the meat golden brown. Veal must always be thoroughly done. Serve with gravy or tomato sauce.

MEMORANDA

MEMORANDA

FRYING

FRYING is one of the most useful methods of cooking, especially of recooking or reheating such small combinations as rissoles, croquettes and small, made dishes which hardly need more than heating through, and browning for the sake of giving them an attractive appearance. It is, however, one of the least understood methods of cooking as well as one of the most poorly performed; hence the discredit into which it has fallen.

The difference between frying and sautéing should be clearly understood. The former needs sufficient fat to completely immerse the article to be fried; the latter requires only a little fat in the pan, but despite the seeming extravagance of "plenty of fat", the former is, for most foods, the better and more digestible form of preparation.

The very best medium for all frying is olive oil, but the price is prohibitive to most people.

Cottonseed oil, if properly refined and carefully used, comes next, but it requires care to avoid unpleasant odor from overheating and, again, many persons object to cotton oil because they have eaten food carelessly prepared with it.

Lard is most commonly used, but is considered by many to be unhealthful. It seems, therefore, that the frying medium likely to be pleasing to all and free from most objections is good beef drippings which can be clarified at home, a rule for which is given on page 31.

Cast steel or aluminum pans should be used as they retain the steady temperature required for frying. They should be fairly deep, and have straight sides. A frying basket made of wire mesh is exceedingly convenient where much frying is done. The advantage of the basket is that several articles can be lowered into and raised from the fat at one time, and the risk of breaking the food in lifting it from

the fat is lessened. A wire dipper or spoon must
be provided if there is no frying basket.

The temperature of frying-fat is very important.
As few cooks possess a fryometer the following sim-
ple tests will serve to decide when fat is at the proper
heat for the purpose desired:

For foods that have been previously cooked and
need only reheating and browning, the fat should
be so hot that a faint blue vapor is seen rising from
it when the pan is held against the light. This
applies when animal fat is used. Oil need not be
quite so hot, and should be tested by frying a small
piece of crust in it. If this quickly turns brown,
the fat is hot; but if slow to take color, heat a little
longer before beginning to fry.

Doughnuts and crullers, being heavy and solid as
compared with croquettes or other small fried foods,
should be cooked in fat at a lower temperature.
The best test is to put a small piece of dough in the
pan and cook it. If it sinks to the bottom and almost immediately reappears, increases in bulk and
slowly browns, the remainder of the dough should
be cooked. Do not attempt to cook too many
crullers or doughnuts at one time as they cool the
fat and, consequently, absorb grease; four or five
are the most that should be cooked at one time.
Drain as soon as done, on unglazed paper as this
absorbs grease; then sprinkle with sugar or shake
them with a little sugar in a paper bag.

After frying any dough mixture the fat will appear
cloudy from the flour that has fallen into it, but if
a few raw potatoes are cooked in the fat the cloudi-
ness will disappear.

Fat should always be strained through a fine sieve
or cheese cloth after using, to remove any foreign
particles that have fallen into it from the food. If
not removed these will burn and probably spoil the
fat.

To prepare meats, fish and croquettes for frying
they should be coated with egg and bread crumbs.
For this beat one egg yolk and white together and

add a tablespoon of water, partly to thin it and
partly to increase the bulk. Have ready on a paper
or plate plenty of fine bread crumbs. Do not use
cracker crumbs if it can be avoided as they absorb
grease and do not give as pleasing a color.

Having trimmed and shaped the article to be fried,
lay it in the beaten egg and with a small brush
cover it completely; lift with the blade of a knife
and place upside down in the bread crumbs. If the
knife blade has displaced any of the egg, brush over
again. Toss in the crumbs till completely covered,
then shake off those which are loose that they may
not fall off in the fat and burn. Continue till all
are coated, then pass the remaining crumbs through
a sieve and put away till needed again.

To prepare Beef Fat for Frying. Buy four pounds of
soft flank fat, or "cod fat" as it is sometimes called;
do not get suet as it is too hard and also costs more
than the flank fat. Cut into pieces the size of an
English walnut and remove all flesh and gristle.
Put into a large pan with a pint of water and cook
fast, without a cover, till all the water has evaporated, when the liquid in the pan will be clear and
like honey. As long as there is water remaining it
will be thick and milky looking. Now cover the
saucepan, and cook very gently till the pieces of skin
and fat cells float on top of the clear fat. Strain
and use for all frying, either plain or mixed with
lard. If these directions are carefully followed the
fat will be good as long as there is any remaining.

MEMORANDA

MEMORANDA

MEMORANDA

POULTRY

POULTRY should be cleaned and dressed as soon as possible after being killed. Pinfeathers are best removed with a small knife or by the aid of a tong-shaped strawberry huller.

To draw the tendons from the drumstick, make an incision lengthwise between the bones of the leg, below the joint, while the foot is still attached to the body. Next, take a strong, thin skewer and pick up the tendons, one at a time, through the incision; hold the skewer, with the tendon on it, with the first two fingers and give a vigorous pull. The tendon should come out easily, and the process can be repeated till all are removed. There are seven small and two large tendons. If these are removed the drumstick is likely to be as tender as any portion of the bird.

The feet may now be cut off a little below the joint, and long hairs on the body removed by singeing. Do this by holding it over a burner of the gas range or by applying a lighted taper or twist of lighted paper. The former method is the better one, as there is no danger of smoking the skin.

To remove the down from a duck or goose, rub over with two teaspoons of alcohol, lay the bird in a dish or pan and set fire to the alcohol. The down will be burned off more quickly and thoroughly than by any other method.

The bird is now ready for drawing and, especially if it is to be roasted, this had better be done at home as the butcher usually makes far too large an opening in the flesh. Make an incision in the skin below the breast bone and with the hand remove the gizzard, heart, intestines and liver, being very careful not to break the gall bag which is attached to

35

the latter, as it would cause the parts with which it comes in contact to taste bitter. Remove the lungs, which lie on either side of the backbone, also the kidneys, windpipe and crop. The latter is reached by inserting the fingers under the skin of the neck after the head is cut off. The oil bag found at the base of the tail must also be removed. Wipe the bird well both inside and out. If there seems to be any indication that it has been kept too long, wash with water in which a little soda has been dissolved and put a small piece of charcoal in the body to absorb any possible odor.

To Truss a Fowl. Draw the legs up close to the body and fasten in place with a skewer run through both drumsticks and the body. Do the same with the wings, skewering them so that they lie flat to the body. Cut the neck off close, fold the skin of the neck under and fasten it down with a small skewer. Cut a slit in the skin just above that made for the removal of the intestines, and pull the tail through this slit, fastening it in place with a long string, that the opening may be concealed. Now take the same string and twist it around the ends of the skewer that holds the legs; cross the string over the back of the bird and fasten to the other skewer, so as to hold all four joints in place and keep them from slipping.

To Prepare a Bird for Broiling. Remove tendons and pinfeathers as directed in rule for preparation of poultry. With a sharp knife split the bird full length down the back, remove insides as before described, wipe, and before cooking cut through the wing and leg joints to simplify serving the bird at table.

Dressing for Roast Chicken. Some claim that a stuffed chicken is a spoiled chicken and that the dressing absorbs much of the moisture and flavor from the flesh. If preferred, the dressing may be cooked separately and served with the bird.

Chestnut Dressing

1½ pounds French chest-   1 cup stale bread crumbs.
  nuts.   ½ cup scalded milk.
⅓ cup butter.   Salt and pepper to taste.

Remove the shells from the nuts and blanch by pouring boiling water over them; allow them to stand five minutes when the brown skin can be removed with the fingers and a knife. Cook the nuts in boiling salted water till tender, which will probably take about half an hour; mash finely, add the butter and seasoning, also the crumbs which have had the scalded milk poured over them. Mix well, and use for stuffing either chicken or turkey.

Plain Dressing for Chicken or Turkey

1 cup stale bread crumbs   Grated rind of half a lemon.
  or pieces of bread.   1 teaspoon mixed herbs.
1 tablespoon chopped   ⅓ cup melted butter or suet.
  parsley.   Salt and pepper.
        ½ cup scalding water or milk.

Crumble the bread finely, add the parsley, lemon rind, herbs, salt and pepper. Chop the suet and add to the other ingredients; or if butter is used, melt it in the water or milk and add, mixing well. Fill the body of the bird with the dressing.

For stuffing turkey double all the ingredients.

Sage and Onion Dressing

10 good-sized onions.   1 teaspoon powdered sage.
1½ cups stale bread crumbs. Salt and pepper to taste.

Peel the onions and cook till tender in boiling salted water, pouring off the first water and adding fresh after they have cooked ten minutes, to take away much of the strong taste and odor. When thoroughly cooked, drain and chop the onions finely; add the sage, bread crumbs and seasonings, and use as a stuffing for goose, duck or boned leg of pork. This may be also cooked in a separate tin in the oven and served with the meat, if preferred.

Potato Dressing

3 cups hot mashed potato.
1 cup stale bread crumbs.
1 grated onion.
1 egg.
½ cup finely-chopped salt pork.
1 teaspoon powdered sage.
Salt and pepper to taste.

Mash the potato quite finely, add the bread crumbs, onion, pork, sage, salt and pepper and mix with the egg lightly beaten. Use as a dressing for goose, duck or pork. This dressing is milder than the one previously given.

Chicken Loaf

1 fowl.
2 tablespoons granulated gelatine.
½ cup cold water.
2 hard-cooked eggs.
Seasoning to taste.

Boil a fowl — an old one will do — in sufficient water to cover, till the meat is ready to fall from the bones. Cool the bird, strain, and continue to cook the liquor till it is reduced to three cupfuls.

Remove all skin and bone from the fowl and lay the meat in a mould, light and dark meat alternately, adding the hard-cooked eggs cut in slices. Season the liquor and add to it the granulated gelatine that has been soaked half an hour in a third of a cup of cold water. When thoroughly dissolved, pour the liquor over the meat and set away to harden.

Chicken à la Stanley

¼ cup butter.
1 sliced onion.
1 chicken.
1½ cups water or stock.
1½ tablespoons flour.
½ cup cream.
Salt and pepper to taste.

Melt the butter and in it cook the onion, and chicken — which must be cut in pieces convenient for serving — for ten minutes. Remove the chicken and put in the flour, blend it smoothly with the butter, add stock or water, stir until boiling and then put in the chicken and cook till tender. Add the cream and seasoning just before serving.

Chicken à la Providence

1 chicken.	¼ cup cooked carrot.
2 cups stock.	¼ cup cooked peas.
2 tablespoons butter.	1 teaspoon chopped parsley.
2 tablespoons flour.	2 egg yolks.
	Seasoning.

Boil the chicken gently till tender, seasoning while cooking; cut into pieces convenient for serving and set aside while the sauce is being prepared.

Sauce. Melt the butter, add flour and blend smoothly; add the stock (liquor in which the chicken was cooked) and stir till boiling. Cook five minutes, put in the carrot and peas, also the yolks of eggs and seasoning. Pour over the chicken and sprinkle with chopped parsley.

Italian Chicken

1 chicken.	1 small onion thinly sliced.
1½ pints water.	Seasoning of salt and pepper.
½ cup olive oil.	1 egg yolk.
	2 teaspoons cornstarch.

Cut the chicken into pieces as for a fricassee; cook till tender in just enough water to cover it, adding salt and pepper when about half done. Remove from the pan and let the chicken become quite cold; then dry each piece thoroughly. Heat half a cup of olive oil in a shallow frying-pan, add the onion to it and when smoking hot put in the chicken, a little at a time, and cook golden brown. When it is all cooked, add to the remaining oil a cup and a half of the liquor in which the chicken was cooked, bring to the boiling point and thicken with the cornstarch rubbed smooth with a little cold water. Cook five minutes, and just before serving add the yolk of the egg, and more seasoning if it is required. Pour the sauce over the chicken.

Curried Chicken

4 tablespoons butter.	1 teaspoon onion juice.
3 tablespoons flour.	½ sour apple or 1 table-
1 tablespoon curry powder.	spoon lemon juice.
2 cups milk or chicken	Salt and pepper.
stock.	2 cups chicken cut into dice.

Melt the butter, add flour and curry powder and cook five minutes; then pour in the milk or stock, whichever is to be used, and stir constantly till the sauce boils; add the onion juice (obtained by pressing a cut onion on a grater) and then put in the chicken and seasoning, and heat thoroughly. If apple is used, chop it finely and add as soon as the sauce boils; if lemon is to be the acid ingredient, do not put it into the sauce till the moment of serving. Serve with boiled rice in a separate dish.

Chicken en Casserole

1 young chicken.	A few mushrooms, canned
3 tablespoons butter.	or fresh.
1 small onion.	2 cups stock or water.
1 small carrot.	3 potatoes.
1 bay leaf.	Salt and pepper to taste.

3 tablespoons sherry.

Clean, singe and cut the chicken into pieces convenient for serving. Melt the butter in a small frying-pan, add the onion and carrot, both cut in thin slices, also the pieces of chicken, and cook all till golden brown, placing them in the casserole as they reach this stage. Pour the stock over them, put in the bay leaf, and cover closely.

When nearly done, add the potatoes sliced, the mushrooms and seasoning. Cover, and finish the cooking. Add the sherry at the last moment before serving, and send to table in the casserole.

Chicken Pot Pie

1 chicken.	Water or stock, about 1 quart.
¼ pound pork.	Seasoning.

Dumplings.

Cut the chicken into rather small pieces and the pork into dice. Lay them in a good-sized saucepan,

cover with water or stock and bring to the boiling
point; keep closely covered and simmer from one
to two hours, according to the age of the chicken.
Season when about half done. Put in the dumplings
thirty minutes before serving time, keeping the pan
closely covered till they are done. Pile the meat in
the centre of the dish and arrange the dumplings
around it. Be sure there is plenty of gravy.

Dumplings

1½ cups flour.   1 teaspoon Rumford Baking
½ teaspoon salt.   Powder.
Milk to mix to a soft dough that will just drop from the spoon.

Sift the flour, salt and baking powder together
twice; add the milk (it will probably take about
two-thirds of a cup), mix thoroughly but quickly,
and drop by small tablespoonfuls into the hot gravy.
Cook as directed in rule for Chicken Pot Pie. Some
prefer to cook the dumplings separately and thicken
the chicken gravy with a little flour and butter
rubbed smoothly together.

Pilau of Fowl (an Indian dish)

1 fowl.   1 small onion.
1 quart white stock.   1 cup rice.
¼ cup butter.   Salt and cayenne to taste.
1 ounce sweet almonds.   1 inch stick cinnamon.
12 seeded raisins.   2 cloves.

Clean and truss the fowl and cook in the stock for
one hour. While this is cooking, heat the butter
and fry in it till golden brown, the almonds blanched
and shredded, the onion peeled and sliced, the
raisins, cloves and cinnamon. When brown, remove
these from the pan and fry the rice in the same
butter till golden brown. Drain off the superfluous
butter and add the rice and other ingredients to the
pan containing the chicken and stock. Cook till
rice and chicken are both tender; then place the
whole on one dish and garnish with slices of fried
bacon.

TO ROAST DUCK

A domestic duck requires almost twice as much cooking as a wild duck. The latter should always be rare and will take about thirty minutes in a hot oven. Wild ducks should always have strips of bacon or salt pork laid across the breast while roasting, to keep them moist. Both kinds need thorough basting.

For dressing see recipes for Sage and Onion Dressing or Potato Dressing.

Wild ducks are never stuffed.

Braised Duck

1 good-sized duck — an old one will serve.	1 sliced onion.
	1 bay leaf.
¼ pound fat salt pork.	A little parsley.
1 carrot cut in dice.	Salt and cayenne to taste.

Cut the pork into small pieces and fry; add the vegetables, bay leaf and parsley, and cook five minutes. Put in the duck, either trussed as for roasting or cut into joints. Cook in the fat till browned; then place in a baking-dish or casserole. Pour the vegetables and fat over it and add three cups of boiling water. Cover closely and cook in a moderate oven till tender, adding more water if necessary. Dish the bird, and thicken the gravy with two tablespoonfuls each of flour and butter rubbed smoothly together. Season highly, and serve with currant jelly or apple sauce.

Potted Pigeons

4 pigeons.	1 slice fat salt pork.
1½ pints water or stock.	2 tablespoons butter.
1 stalk of celery.	2 tablespoons flour.
Salt and pepper.	

Clean and truss the birds as for roasting. Cut the pork into dice, try out the fat and brown the birds in it. Put them in a casserole or baking-dish, add the celery, seasoning and stock; cover closely and cook about two hours. Remove the pigeons to the serving dish, and thicken the gravy with the butter and flour rubbed smoothly together. Pour the gravy over the birds, first having removed the celery.

Fried Chicken

1 chicken.	A little cold water.
Salt, pepper and a little flour.	½ cup lard and butter mixed.

Clean the chicken, remove pinfeathers and oil bag, and cut into convenient pieces for serving. Dip each joint into the water and then into the flour, salt and pepper sifted together, shaking off all that does not cling to the chicken. Heat the butter and lard in a frying-pan and cook the pieces of chicken slowly that they may be done through, turning often while cooking. Keep hot till all are done, and serve with white sauce or brown gravy.

Fricassee Chicken

1 good-sized chicken.	Salt and pepper.
1 small onion.	A little chopped parsley.
A few slices of salt pork.	A few mushrooms (these can
2 tablespoons flour.	be omitted).
1 tablespoon butter.	Boiling water to cover.

Cut the chicken into good-sized pieces and wipe with a damp cloth. Cut the pork small and try it out in a saucepan, and when the fat runs freely put in the chicken, a few pieces at a time, and cook till slightly colored, but not browned. Put the tougher parts of the bird at the bottom of the pan, then add the onion and cover with boiling water. Cover closely and cook very slowly till tender, adding the seasoning at the end of an hour. It is not possible to give the exact length of time required for the cooking as some chickens take longer than others.

A few minutes before serving, remove the meat from the pan, and thicken the gravy with the butter and flour rubbed smoothly together. Cook five minutes after adding the thickening, then pour the gravy over and around the chicken. If mushrooms are used, add them when the cooking is about half done. Sprinkle the parsley over the chicken after dishing.

Chicken Mould

1 cup cold chicken.	1 egg.
1 cup chicken stock or ½ stock and half cream or milk.	2 level tablespoons gelatine. Seasoning.

Chop the chicken finely and pass through a sieve; season delicately and. add to it the egg, yolk and white beaten separately, and the stock in which the gelatine has been dissolved. Turn into a mould and, when cold, turn out and slice thinly.

MEMORANDA

MEMORANDA

FISH AND MEAT SAUCES

Oyster Sauce

1 pint of oysters.
3 tablespoons butter.
3 tablespoons flour.

1 cup milk.
Salt, pepper and lemon juice for the seasoning.

Scald the oysters in their own liquor; chop them coarsely and reserve three-fourths cup of the liquor.

Blend the butter and flour in a saucepan without browning, add the milk and oyster liquor and stir till boiling; cook five minutes, add the seasoning and oysters, and cook just long enough to let them get thoroughly hot.

Bechamel Sauce

2 tablespoons butter.
2 tablespoons flour.

1 cup stock.
½ cup cream.
Seasoning to taste.

Melt the butter, add the flour and blend till smooth, without browning. Add the stock a little at a time, stirring constantly till all is used. Cook five minutes, season, and add the cream just before serving.

Mint Sauce

½ cup fresh mint leaves.
⅔ cup vinegar.

2 tablespoons sugar.

Wash the mint well before stripping the leaves from the stalks, dry thoroughly and chop finely. Add the vinegar and sugar, and let the sauce stand till the sugar is dissolved. Serve with roast lamb.

Cucumber Sauce

2 cucumbers.
½ teaspoon onion juice.

2 tablespoons olive oil.
1 tablespoon vinegar.
Salt and pepper to taste.

Peel the cucumbers and either grate or chop them finely; drain well to get rid of all the moisture pos-

47

sible and add the onion juice, oil, vinegar and seasonings beaten together. Serve as soon as made.
This sauce is good with either broiled or fried
fish, or cold meats.

Mushroom Sauce

1½ tablespoons butter.	1 bay leaf.
2 tablespoons flour.	1 slice onion.
1½ cups brown stock.	1 cup mushrooms.

Cook the butter and flour together till brown, add
the stock, onion and bay leaf, and cook ten minutes.
Remove the bay leaf and onion and add the mushrooms. If canned mushrooms are used cut them in
halves; if fresh ones, they must be peeled, coarsely
chopped and cooked five minutes in a little butter
before adding to the sauce. Season and serve.

Maître d'Hôtel Sauce

½ cup butter.	1 tablespoon lemon juice.
10 drops onion juice.	1 tablespoon chopped parsley.
	Salt and pepper.

Beat the butter to a cream as for a cake, add
the lemon juice a little at a time and, when well
blended, stir in the parsley, onion juice and seasoning. Form into a ball or flat cake and set aside to
chill before serving.

Béarnaise Sauce

4 egg yolks.	1 tablespoon of plain or
4 tablespoons oil or melted	tarragon vinegar.
butter.	2 tablespoons hot water.
	Salt and pepper.

Put the well-beaten yolks of eggs in a bowl and
stand this in a saucepan of hot water over the fire.
Add the oil or butter very gradually, stirring all the
time. Next pour in the two tablespoonfuls of hot
water and continue to stir till thick and smooth.
Remove at once from the heat and add the vinegar,

salt and pepper. This sauce needs most careful watching while being made.

Horseradish Sauce

2 tablespoons butter.	Salt, pepper and lemon juice.
2 tablespoons flour.	2 level tablespoons grated
1½ cups milk or fish stock,	horseradish.
or part of each.	1 egg yolk.

Blend the butter and flour in a saucepan till smooth, add the liquid, a little at a time, and stir till boiling. Season with the salt, pepper and lemon juice and cook a few minutes. Just before serving, add the horseradish and yolk of the egg. If grated horseradish can not be obtained, add one teaspoon of evaporated horseradish which has been soaked for a few minutes in a tablespoon of cold water.

Piquante Sauce

1 small onion.	1 teaspoon chopped parsley.
2 tablespoons butter.	1 teaspoon made mustard.
2 tablespoons flour.	A little chopped cucumber
1 cup stock.	pickle.
1 teaspoon vinegar.	Salt and pepper to taste.

Melt and heat the butter in a saucepan, add the onion, chopped small, and fry golden brown in the butter; then put in the flour and stir till perfectly smooth; add the stock slowly and stir till boiling. Cook five minutes, season, and add the vinegar, mustard, parsley and pickle.
Serve with boiled or baked fish.

Tartare Sauce

1 cup mayonnaise dressing.	1 teaspoon finely-chopped
(Recipe given under	capers.
"Salad Dressings.")	1 teaspoon finely-chopped
1 teaspoon made mustard.	pickles.
1 teaspoon finely-chopped	½ teaspoon onion juice.
parsley.	

Add all the ingredients to the mayonnaise in the order given; stir well and serve very cold.

Tomato Sauce

½ can tomatoes.	Salt and pepper.
½ a small onion.	1 bay leaf.
1 sprig parsley.	2 tablespoons butter
	2 tablespoons flour.

Put together in a saucepan the tomatoes, onion, parsley and bay leaf; cook gently for twenty minutes, then rub through a sieve. Press all the pulp possible through the sieve and scrape off all that clings to the under side. Melt the butter in another pan, add the flour, and when these are smooth add the strained tomato slowly, stirring constantly to prevent the sauce being lumpy. Cook five minutes after the sauce boils; add seasoning, and serve.

Some cooks add a little sugar to the sauce to neutralize the acid. One-sixth teaspoon bicarbonate of soda dissolved in a teaspoon of cold water and added to the sauce will serve the same purpose.

Parsley Sauce

2 tablespoons butter.	1 teaspoon lemon juice.
2 tablespoons flour.	Salt and pepper to taste.
1 cup milk.	2 tablespoons chopped parsley.

Put the butter and flour together in a saucepan, and blend thoroughly without coloring. Add the milk, a little at a time, stirring constantly till the sauce boils. Cook five minutes; add the salt, pepper and lemon juice and, just before serving, the chopped parsley.

To Prepare the Parsley. Wash and dry thoroughly and remove all stalks. Chop finely and wash again, placing the chopped parsley in the corner of a cloth and twisting the cloth that none may escape, then hold under the water faucet and press the parsley with the thumb and finger to get rid of the excess of green coloring matter liberated by the chopping; otherwise this would make the sauce a dull, rather dirty-looking color, instead of perfectly white with minute particles of green parsley distributed through it.

MEMORANDA

MEMORANDA

ENTRÉES AND CHEESE DISHES

Ham and Macaroni Scallop

18 sticks of macaroni.	1 cup milk.
1 cup minced ham.	¼ teaspoon pepper.
2 tablespoons butter.	2 tablespoons grated cheese.
1 tablespoon flour.	½ cup stale bread crumbs.

1 tablespoon butter.

Break the macaroni into short lengths and cook it in boiling salted water till tender, which will probably take about thirty minutes.

Make a sauce by blending the butter and flour smoothly, adding the milk and stirring till the mixture boils; then add the pepper, but no salt as the ham will sufficiently salt the mixture. Grease a baking-dish and place in it alternate layers of macaroni, ham and sauce, sprinkling a little of the cheese over each layer of the macaroni. Melt the other tablespoon of butter, add the crumbs to it, and stir till they have absorbed the butter. Spread over the ingredients in the dish, and bake till golden brown.

Fricassee of Liver

2 pounds calf's liver.	1 small onion.
½ pound fat salt pork.	1 tablespoon chopped
1 tablespoon butter or	parsley.
drippings.	Salt and pepper to taste.

Cut the liver into rather thick slices and the pork into dice. Melt the butter in the upper part of a double boiler, lay the slices of liver in it, and put in the diced pork; slice the onion and add with the parsley and seasoning. Cover closely and set the saucepan over the lower part of the boiler which contains boiling water, place at the back of the range where it will keep hot, without boiling, for an hour; then increase the heat and cook an hour longer. Thicken the gravy with a tablespoon each of butter and flour rubbed smoothly together, and serve very hot.

53

Meat Fritters

1 cup finely-chopped cold meat: beef, lamb or chicken, etc.	1 tablespoon chopped parsley. 1 cup flour. 1 egg.
Salt, pepper and a little onion juice, lemon, mint or other flavoring.	1 teaspoon Rumford Baking Powder. 1 cup milk. Frying fat.

Season the meat to taste, varying the seasoning according to the kind of meat. For chicken a little lemon rind may be added, and for lamb a little finely-chopped mint; add the parsley in either case. Make a batter with the flour, baking powder, egg and milk, to which add the seasoned meat, and drop by spoonfuls into the hot fat. Fry golden brown and drain well. Serve hot with or without a sauce or gravy.

Corned Beef Croquettes

2 tablespoons butter. 2 tablespoons mashed potato. ¼ cup cream. 1½ cups finely-chopped corned beef.	2 tablespoons chopped parsley. 1 well-beaten egg. Egg and bread crumbs. Pepper to taste. Salt (if necessary).

Melt the butter in a saucepan, add the mashed potato and cream, and heat thoroughly. Next, put in the meat, parsley and seasoning, and, lastly, the beaten egg. Spread the mixture on a plate and when cool shape into croquettes, either in the form of large corks or a cone; coat with beaten egg and bread crumbs, and fry golden brown in smoking-hot fat.

Blanquette of Veal

1¼ tablespoons butter. 1½ tablespoons flour. 1 cup stock. ½ cup cream.	2 cups cooked veal cut into dice. 12 mushrooms. 2 egg yolks.
	Seasoning.

Blend the butter and flour together without browning; add the stock and cream, and cook till the sauce thickens. Put in the meat and mush-rooms (canned ones will do), and heat. Just before serving stir in the egg yolks and cook one minute. Season, and serve very hot.

Veal Klopps

2 cups finely-minced veal.	Salt and pepper to taste.
Juice of 1 small onion.	A little grated lemon rind.
The unbeaten whites of 3 eggs.	

Add the onion juice, seasoning and lemon rind to the minced veal, and form a paste of the seasoned meat with the whites of eggs. Shape with the hands into very small balls and, when all are ready, drop a few at a time into boiling salted water in a shallow pan and cook gently for five minutes. Serve on rounds of buttered toast. Cover with either a tomato sauce or rich white sauce.

Chicken Livers with Bacon

1 dozen livers.	Seasoning of salt, pepper and
Slices of bacon.	lemon juice.

Clean the livers (carefully remove the gall bag if this has not already been done), and cut them in halves, wrapping each piece in a slice of thinly cut bacon. Secure the bacon with a small skewer or wooden toothpick; lay on a broiler and place in a baking-pan to catch the fat. Cook in a hot oven till the bacon is crisp, turning once or twice during the cooking. Season, and sprinkle with lemon juice before serving.

Chicken Chartreuse

2 cups cold boiled rice.	A little grated lemon rind.
1½ cups minced chicken.	Salt and pepper to taste.
1 tablespoon chopped parsley.	Cream sauce or gravy.

Grease a plain mould and line throughout with rice, pressing it with a spoon to make sure it clings. Add the parsley and lemon rind to the minced chicken, with salt and pepper to taste, and fill the hollow inside the lining of rice with the seasoned meat. Cover with a little more rice, and steam three-quarters of an hour. Turn onto a hot dish, and cover completely with sauce or gravy.

Stuffed Peppers

1½ cups cold cooked chicken.
Salt, pepper and a little grated lemon rind.
½ pint chopped oysters with their liquor.

½ cup stale bread crumbs.
2 tablespoons melted butter.
1 teaspoon minced parsley.
6 green peppers.

Mince the chicken finely; add the salt, pepper and lemon rind, also the oysters, butter, crumbs and parsley. Cut a slice from the stem end of the peppers, remove all the seeds and white fibre, and fill with the chicken mixture. Bake half an hour in a moderate oven. Tomatoes may be stuffed with the same filling, if desired.

Broiled Sweetbreads

1 pair sweetbreads.
Juice of half a lemon.

2 tablespoons butter.
Salt and cayenne.

Put the sweetbreads in cold water and let them stand an hour; then drain and place in a saucepan containing a pint of boiling water, the juice of half a lemon and a little salt. Cook gently for twenty minutes and again plunge into cold water that the sweetbreads may be white and firm. Dry, split, season lightly and broil over a clear fire about five minutes. Serve very hot with maître d'hôtel sauce.

Cheese Puffs

2 well-beaten eggs.
¾ cup flour.
½ cup grated cheese.
Salt and pepper to taste.

1 teaspoon Rumford Baking Powder.
1 scant cup of milk.
Frying fat.

Beat the eggs well and add the milk. Sift together the flour, baking powder and seasoning; add the cheese and mix to a stiff batter with the milk and eggs. Beat well, and drop by spoonfuls into hot fat. Fry golden brown, drain and serve.

Cheese Patties

A little plain paste.
2 tablespoons butter.
2 small eggs.
½ cup bread crumbs.
½ cup grated cheese.
1 teaspoon Rumford Baking Powder.
⅓ cup milk.
Salt and cayenne to taste.

Roll the paste thinly, cut out, and line small tins. Beat the butter to a cream, add the eggs slightly beaten, bread crumbs, cheese, baking powder and seasoning; mix with the milk, and put a spoonful in each tin. Bake about fifteen minutes in a hot oven.

Escalloped Cheese

2 cups stale bread cut into dice.
1 cup grated cheese.
1 pint milk.
2 eggs.
Salt and pepper to taste.

Put the bread and cheese into a baking-dish, in alternate layers, until the dish is about two-thirds full. Beat the eggs and add to the milk with the seasoning — not forgetting that cheese is sometimes quite salt — and pour over the cheese and bread. Bake half an hour in a moderate oven.

Cheese Toast

1 tablespoon butter.
1½ tablespoons flour.
Salt and cayenne.
1 cup milk.
1 cup grated cheese.
Slices of buttered toast.

Make the toast first and keep it hot while preparing the sauce. Melt the butter, add the flour and blend smoothly; season, and put in the milk a little at a time, stirring constantly. After cooking five minutes put in the cheese and, when melted, pour over the toast, and place in a hot oven for five minutes before serving.

Deviled Cheese

1½ cups grated cheese.	1 teaspoon Worcestershire
2 tablespoons olive oil.	sauce.
2 tablespoons vinegar.	Salt and pepper to taste.
1 teaspoon dry mustard.	Crackers.

Mix the cheese, mustard, salt and pepper; add the oil, beat until creamy and then mix in the vinegar and sauce. Spread on hot, toasted crackers, or on ordinary crackers or toast, and heat for five minutes in a quick oven.

Macaroni au Gratin

⅓ pound macaroni.	6 tablespoons grated cheese.
1 cup white sauce.	Salt and pepper to taste.

Break the macaroni into convenient lengths and cook in boiling salted water till tender, which will take from half to three-quarters of an hour. Drain thoroughly, and put a layer at the bottom of a deep baking-dish.

Make the sauce by blending in a saucepan three level tablespoons of butter with the same quantity of flour; add slowly one and one-half cups of milk and stir till the sauce boils. Cook three minutes and season with salt and pepper.

Add two-thirds of the cheese to the sauce, and put a layer over the macaroni in the dish. Proceed in this way, first macaroni, then sauce, till the dish is full, having sauce for the last layer. Sprinkle the remainder of the cheese over the top. Bake in a moderate oven about three-quarters of an hour.

Swedish Timbales

¾ cup flour.	1 egg.
½ teaspoon salt.	½ cup milk.
1 teaspoon sugar.	1 tablespoon olive oil.

Sift together the flour, salt and sugar, and mix to a smooth batter with the egg, milk and oil. Let the mixture stand an hour before using. Heat a timbale iron in hot frying-fat and dip it into the batter,

taking care not to allow the batter to come over the
top of the iron. Lower the iron into hot fat and fry
golden brown. It is best to have the batter in a
cup when dipping the timbale iron into it. If the
iron is either too hot or too cold, the batter will
drop off. It is only by practice that the right heat
can be judged.

Mushroom Filling for Timbales

2 cups mushrooms cut in small pieces.	1 tablespoon cornstarch or flour.
3 tablespoons butter.	1 cup cream or milk.
Salt and pepper to taste.	1 tablespoon sherry.

Cook the mushrooms in the butter till tender, add
the salt, pepper and flour or cornstarch, mix smoothly
and put in the cream or milk; stir till boiling and
then cook five minutes longer. At the moment of
serving add the sherry and fill the timbale cases.

Sweetbread and Mushroom Filling

¼ pound mushrooms.	1½ cups milk, or milk and cream.
3 tablespoons butter.	
2 tablespoons flour.	1 sweetbread.

Salt, pepper and a little Worcestershire sauce for seasoning.

Cook the mushrooms in the butter till tender, add
the flour and, when smoothly blended, the milk and
cream. Stir till boiling, and cook five minutes.
Add the sweetbread, which has been cooked and
cut into dice, to the other ingredients, with the seasoning, and fill the timbale cases just before serving.

Oyster Filling

3 tablespoons butter.	1 cup milk and cream mixed.
3 tablespoons flour.	Salt and pepper.
1 pint solid oysters.	1 teaspoon of lemon juice.

Scald the oysters in their own liquor after picking
them over carefully. Blend the butter and flour in

a saucepan till smooth, add the milk and cream slowly, and stir till boiling. Cook five minutes and then put in the oysters with as much of the liquor as will make the sauce the consistency of thick cream. Season, add the lemon juice, and fill the timbale cases just before serving. Either of these three fillings may be served on toast instead of in the timbale cases.

MEMORANDA

MEMORANDA

VEGETABLES

THE usual method of cooking vegetables in a large quantity of water, which is afterwards thrown away, is not to be recommended, as it means the loss of much valuable saline matter as well as sugar.

Where the cooking liquor is not used, with such vegetables as peas, turnips, beans, etc., it is well to add a little sugar while cooking, to replace that which is lost. Root vegetables are all improved by the addition of a little butter when being served.

It is difficult to give a definite time for the cooking of either root or green vegetables, as it depends largely on their age and freshness. Cook all green vegetables rapidly, putting them, after washing, into boiling salted water. Cook without a cover as this preserves the color. Some cooks attain this end by putting a little soda in the water, but this is not advisable. As soon as tender, remove from the water because too much cooking causes the flavor to deteriorate.

The exception to the rule of cooking green vegetables in boiling water is spinach, which requires no water other than that which clings to the leaves after washing.

Cabbage, Cauliflower, Dandelion and Beet Greens, wash thoroughly, remove dead leaves and stand in cold, salted water for an hour. This removes any insects that may be hidden among the leaves. Cabbage is usually cut into quarters when being cleaned; cauliflower is sometimes divided into small flower stalks, and when this is not done it is wise to make a cross-cut in the stalk; otherwise, being hard, it is not likely to be sufficiently cooked as soon as the rest of the plant.

Spinach requires more washing than any other vegetable, because it grows in a sandy soil, close to the ground. Remove roots and dead leaves, then wash by placing in a large vessel of cold water, toss about and then transfer to fresh water. Repeat this process till all sand is removed and the last water is quite clear — from six to ten washings are usually required.

Beets need no preparation before cooking, and must be boiled without even cleaning. The tops should be cut off several inches above the beets and the beets cooked till tender in boiling water; young beets require cooking about an hour, old ones several hours.

Summer Squash may be cooked without peeling if very young, but if the skin is at all likely to be tough, it should be removed. Drain the squash very thoroughly after cooking; or put it in a cloth and wring the ends in opposite directions.

Hubbard Squash may be baked, boiled or steamed, the former being the better method as it leaves the squash drier.

To Bake Squash. Cut it into large pieces, place skin side up in a baking-pan and cook till tender. Scrape the flesh from the skin, and season to taste.

Eggplant should be cut into thick slices, dipped in beaten egg and bread crumbs and fried in a little drippings or bacon fat.

To Stuff and Bake Eggplant. Boil it for half an hour, then cut in halves, scoop out the fleshy part, chop finely, mix with half its bulk of bread crumbs, a little onion juice, chopped parsley or any other seasoning desired; replace the mixture in the shell and bake the whole three-quarters of an hour. A little drippings or butter put over the top of the filling before baking is an improvement. Serve plain or with brown gravy.

Asparagus should be scraped and the tough part of the stalk removed; then tied in bunches and cooked till tender in boiling salted water.

Green Corn should be cooked as soon as possible after gathering. Remove the husk and silky fibre and break the ears if too long to go into the kettle easily; cook in boiling water just long enough to thicken the milk of the grain — from twelve to twenty-five minutes will be required, according to the age of the corn. If it can not be cooked as soon as gathered, leave the husk on till the last moment as it prevents the corn drying and becoming tough.

Peas should have fresh-looking, well-filled, crisp pods. They should not be shelled till just before cooking and will have a richer flavor if some of the pods are cooked in the water. Have the water boiling and cook the peas about twenty minutes. Fresh peas are more tender and seem to be more easily digested than dried ones, but the latter, partly owing to the evaporation of water in the drying process, are, pound for pound, more nutritious and nitrogenous.

All fresh vegetables should be crisp and firm when put on the fire to cook, and if for any reason this crispness is lacking, it may be restored by soaking in very cold water. This soaking may be necessary for a few minutes only, but in extreme cases it will take several hours to attain the desired result.

In cooking all green vegetables it is better to have the saucepan only partly covered, to permit the escape of some of the volatile matter liberated by heat; it also insures a better color. Green vegetables are sometimes prepared for the table by blanching, that is, cooking in fast-boiling water from five to twenty minutes, having the saucepan uncovered, the time required depending on the vegetable. The water is then drained off and cooking completed with the addition of a little butter or drippings, seasoning and, in the case of very dry vegetables, a little stock or water. The saucepan should be covered and the cooking done very gently. Vegetables are better flavored when cooked by this process than when simply boiled in a large quantity of water.

Few cooks realize the importance of cooking fresh vegetables as soon as possible after preparing them. Statistics show that in the case of potatoes, peeled and left soaking in water for several hours, the loss in nitrogenous matter was 50 per cent, and in mineral matter 40 per cent; while when placed at once in boiling water after peeling, they lost only 8 per cent and 19 per cent respectively, during the cooking.

Steamed vegetables lose only about one-third as much food value as when immersed in boiling water, but more fuel is used as they cook more slowly.

The greatest changes that occur when cooking vegetables are the swelling and bursting of starch grains, softening of cellular tissue and development of flavors and odors; while if the cooking is too long continued, flavor and odor are partly or entirely lost.

There are several ways of eliminating, at least, a part of the odor of cooking vegetables. One, to discard the first cooking-water after five minutes and replacing it with fresh; another, to place a small piece of charcoal in the pan with the vegetables; or with onions or greens cook a slice of red pepper, fresh or dried, in the pan.

Potatoes should always be kept in a cool, dark place. In warmth and light they are liable to sprout, which is undesirable. They are so commonly used that we might expect them served in perfection, but in reality few vegetables are so poorly cooked. If potatoes are peeled before cooking, it should be done as thinly as possible; the flavor is better and the food value greater if the skin is left on. Always cook potatoes of even size at one time that all may be done together.

Baking is the best method of cooking, as all the potash salts are retained and dry heat bursts the starch cells, rendering the potatoes mealy and digestible. When baked or boiled in their skins they must be eaten as soon as cooked, otherwise the flavor changes quickly. If delay is necessary, break the skin to let some of the moisture escape.

To boil potatoes, either in their jackets or when peeled, put them into enough boiling water to cover, add a tablespoon of salt for each dozen potatoes, cover the saucepan closely, and if of moderate size cook thirty minutes — small ones may take a little less time. Test with a fork and, if tender, drain at once, let the steam pass off and shake the potatoes in the pan to make them floury. If they can not be served at once, cover lightly with cheese cloth to prevent the cold air reaching them.

Creamed or escalloped potatoes are better prepared from left-over baked ones rather than boiled, as they are drier and of better flavor. The same applies to German fried, that is, cold cooked potatoes fried; also to Lyonnaise potatoes, that is, potatoes fried with minced onion, or chives and chopped parsley.

Savory Potatoes

6 moderate-sized potatoes.	1 pint milk.
2 small onions.	Salt and pepper to taste.

Pare and cut the potatoes in thin slices; put a layer of them in a baking-dish, sprinkle with finely-minced onion, salt and pepper, repeating in the same order till the dish is full or the ingredients all used. Pour enough milk over the potatoes to cover them, and bake slowly till tender, adding more milk as that in the dish boils away.

Hashed Brown Potatoes

6 cold cooked potatoes, baked or boiled.	½ cup salt pork cut in dice and measured after cutting, or ⅓ cup butter.
Salt and pepper to taste.	

Try out the salt pork, and when the fat is given off remove the scraps, or melt the butter and let it become quite hot without browning, — do not use both pork and butter, — put the potatoes into the fat and toss them about till hot; season, then let them remain in the pan without stirring till the under side is browned. Invert on a hot dish that the browned side may be uppermost.

Potato Croquettes

2 cups mashed potato.	2 teaspoons chopped parsley.
1 tablespoon butter.	½ teaspoon onion juice.
Salt, pepper and a little celery salt.	1 egg.

Pass the potato through a potato ricer or sieve to insure all lumps being removed. This is best done when the potatoes are freshly boiled and hot. Add and beat in the butter, seasoning, parsley and onion juice, and when these are well mixed stir in the well-beaten egg, or as much of it as is required to make the potato just firm enough to handle easily. Form into croquettes of any desired shape, dip in beaten egg and bread crumbs (see instructions for Frying, page 30), and cook golden brown in hot fat.

Lyonnaise Potatoes

6 cold cooked potatoes, baked or boiled.	2 medium-sized onions.
	2 tablespoons butter.
Salt and pepper to taste.	

Peel and cut the potatoes into slices, peel and thinly slice the onions. Heat the butter and fry the onions in it till they just begin to turn yellow; then put in the potatoes and seasoning, and cook golden brown, turning the potatoes about constantly in the pan that they may cook and color evenly.

Creole Tomatoes

4 large tomatoes.	Salt and cayenne.
1 small onion.	4 tablespoons butter.
2 green peppers, finely chopped.	1 tablespoon flour.
	1 cup milk and cream.

Cut the tomatoes in halves crosswise; lay cut side up in a baking-pan and sprinkle with the finely-

chopped onion, also the peppers from which the
seeds and veins have been removed. Season highly,
put a small piece of butter on each piece of tomato,
using two tablespoonfuls for the purpose. Pour half
a cup of water into the pan, and bake in a quick
oven till the tomatoes are tender. Melt the remaining two tablespoons of butter and brown the flour
in it; add milk and cream, also the liquor from the
baking-pan, stir till boiling and cook three minutes
longer. Dish the tomatoes on squares of toast and
pour the sauce around them.

Escalloped Cauliflower

1 cauliflower.	½ cup bread crumbs.
1 tablespoon butter.	½ cup nuts.
½ cup cream.	Salt and pepper.
	1 cup milk.

Cook the cauliflower in boiling salted milk and
water till tender, using the milk to keep the cauliflower white; drain, and break the vegetable into
small pieces. Heat the butter and cream together
and add seasoning and nuts. Grease a baking-dish
and sprinkle it with crumbs; put in a layer of cauliflower, then a little of the sauce, more cauliflower
and more sauce, till the dish is filled or the ingredients used. Sprinkle the remainder of the crumbs
on top, and place in a hot oven to brown.

Creamed Celery

The outside stalks of 3	2 tablespoons flour.
heads of celery.	1½ cups milk.
2 tablespoons butter.	Salt and pepper to taste.

Wash and scrape the celery and cut into inch
lengths; cook in salted water till tender, which will
probably require about half an hour, and then drain
very thoroughly. Blend together the butter and
flour, add the milk a little at a time, stirring constantly till the whole boils. Cook three minutes,

add salt and pepper, and heat the celery in the sauce. Onions, parsnips and carrots may be prepared in the same manner.

Hashed Turnip

1 large yellow turnip.	¼ teaspoon pepper.
2 tablespoons butter.	1 tablespoon chopped
1 level teaspoon salt.	parsley.
¼ cup thin cream.	

Peel the turnip thickly and cut into dice. Cook till tender in boiling water, then drain and return to the saucepan; add the butter, seasoning, parsley and cream. Let the whole boil up once, and serve.

Corn Oysters

½ pint grated green corn.	1 egg.
2 tablespoons flour.	½ cup milk.
½ teaspoon salt.	Butter.

Scrape or grate the corn from the cob. Sift the flour and salt and mix to a batter with the egg and milk; stir the corn into the batter and drop by spoonfuls into a frying-pan containing a little hot butter. When one side is brown turn and cook the other.

MEMORANDA

MEMORANDA

SALADS

SALADS AND SALAD DRESSINGS

ALMOST every variety of vegetables and fruits may be made into salads. Eggs are used also, as well as many kinds of fish and meat. Vegetable salads are the most common and should therefore receive first consideration.

Naturally, lettuce heads the list. It is more popular because we can get it when other vegetables are almost unobtainable. The round, close heads are more generally used than the long-leaf variety. Curly lettuce, while pretty, is tougher than either of the other two. Lettuce contains little nutriment, but is rich in mineral salts.

Sorrel is one of the wild salad plants and deserves to be better known and appreciated. It has a slightly acid taste, and for this reason be sparing of the vinegar when dressing it. Sorrel may be used as a salad by itself, or blended with other salad plants such as lettuce or spinach.

Mustard and cress used together make a good salad.

Small yellow tomatoes dipped for a moment in boiling water, then peeled with a sharp knife, thoroughly chilled, seasoned, sprinkled with chopped parsley, piled on lettuce leaves and served with a French dressing make a salad that tastes as good as it looks.

In winter, when fresh salad plants are hard to obtain, a tomato jelly or salad made from canned or fresh (cooked) string beans, or even from the remains of baked beans seasoned with parsley and onion juice, is economical and satisfying.

THE CLEANSING OF SALAD PLANTS

Lettuce. Growing so near the ground much dirt gets into lettuce. In preparing it for the table, separate all the leaves and wash well; the leaves

73

may be left in water about half an hour to absorb moisture and become crisp, but should then be drained in one of the globe-shaped baskets made for the purpose, or dried in a soft cloth. If to be kept for any length of time, wrap the lettuce in damp cheese cloth and place near, but not on, the ice.

Water Cress. This plant requires very careful attention when being prepared for the table, as many non-edible leaves are gathered with it, also because small water insects cling closely to it. A little salt in the water in which the cress is washed will greatly aid their removal.

Endive, Field Salad and Dandelion. These leaves must be carefully picked over, foreign matter removed, and after freshening in water for a short time, well drained before using.

Celery and Chicory. The stalks of these must be broken apart, washed and brushed with a vegetable brush, and all discolored parts cut out. The stalks may remain in water or be wrapped in a damp cloth till used. Only the inner stalks of celery are good for salads; the outer stalks can be boiled and served, with sauce, as a vegetable.

Radishes. These should be washed, scraped and cut in thin slices before being served as a salad.

ALL GREEN SALADS should be chilled before serving that they may be crisp. When the leaves are too large to be served whole they should be broken (not cut) just before sending them to the table. Add dressing to green salads just before eating; if put on sooner it softens the leaves and spoils both taste and appearance. To make a lettuce salad more savory scatter over it before serving a tablespoon of finely-chopped chives or, in their season, the same quantity of chopped green peppers, removing the seeds and white dividing fibre. Peppers and chives may be used together if desired. The salad bowl may be rubbed with a cut onion, or a few drops of onion juice (obtained by pressing a cut onion on a grater) can be added to the salad.

In preparing salads from meat and fish an almost endless variety of flavors can be obtained by careful blending of seasonings to suit the principal ingredient of the salad itself. Few better salads can be eaten than those made from fragments of cold roast lamb cut into dice, mixed with a cup of cooked peas and a little finely-chopped mint. If the lamb be boiled, substitute a few chopped capers for the mint; with cold pork, have a sprinkling of sage and an equal quantity of diced celery; with fish, plenty of lemon juice and cucumber. These salads are all served with a dressing, either French, boiled or mayonnaise as best suits the salad and the convenience of the maker.

FRUIT SALADS are frequently served at luncheon — sometimes as a first course—and may be made of one fruit or a combination of several; those most commonly blended being grapes (skinned and seeded), oranges, grape-fruit, bananas and apples. Serve with French or mayonnaise dressing.

The chief rules to be remembered in making salads are:

1. All salads likely to be dry, as well as those having no dominating flavor, are better if they are marinated with a French dressing some time before serving, in addition to the dressing added at table.

2. It is not enough to wash the salad plants; they must be dried also, for the water dripping from the leaves in the serving dish would thin the dressing and make it insipid.

3. A good portion of the dressing must be mixed with the salad, not all poured over the top.

Harlequin Salad

1 cup each red and white cabbage (shaved).
1 cup French peas.
½ cup beet.

1 diced onion.
⅓ cup diced carrot.
Salt and pepper to season highly.

Have the peas, beet and carrot cooked till tender. Shave the cabbage and cut the onion into very small dice; mix all the vegetables, or, if preferred, arrange them in layers or heaps separately. The effect is better if they are mixed and they are also easier to season and to arrange. Pour a French dressing over the salad an hour before serving, and pass either a mayonnaise or boiled dressing, or a further supply of French dressing, with it at table.

Cheese Salad

½ cup mayonnaise dressing.
½ pound cheese grated or run through a meat chopper.
Celery salt and pepper to taste.
1 dozen capers.
Lettuce.

Mix the mayonnaise with the cheese and add the seasoning. Form into small balls with butter paddles or with two spoons. Serve on lettuce leaves on individual plates, and garnish with the capers. Pass more mayonnaise in a separate dish.

Neufchatel Salad

2 rolls Neufchatel cheese.
2 tablespoons butter.
1 teaspoon each finely-chopped parsley, chives and olives.
Salt and paprika to taste.

Beat the butter and cheese till creamy and well blended; add the parsley, chives, olives and seasoning. Form into small balls and serve on a bed of lettuce or cress with French or mayonnaise dressing.

Potato and Egg Salad

3 eggs.
3 medium-sized potatoes.
Salt and pepper to taste.
French dressing.

Hard cook the eggs, remove shells, and chop finely-using a silver knife to prevent the eggs being discolored. Cook the potatoes, cut into dice while hot and mix with the eggs. Then add the dressing and season with salt and pepper. Serve very cold on a bed of water cress.

Tomato and Lima Bean Salad

4 tomatoes.
1¼ cups cooked Lima beans.
1 tablespoon parsley.

1 very small onion, grated.
½ cup nuts, finely chopped.
2 tablespoons minced celery or a little celery salt.

Salt and pepper to taste.

Cut a slice from the top of each tomato and with a teaspoon remove the pulp. To the beans (if very large, cut in halves) add the onion, parsley, nuts, celery and seasoning. Mix a little French dressing with these ingredients and fill the tomatoes with the mixture. Pour more dressing over the top or serve it separately. Any dressing desired may be served.

The tomatoes may be peeled and cut in thick slices, and the other ingredients piled on them if preferred.

Fruit and Nut Salad

1 large pineapple.
¼ pound shelled almonds.
¼ pound shelled filberts.

1 dozen maraschino cherries.
Lettuce.
Cream or mayonnaise dressing.

Remove the rind and the eyes from the pineapple and cut the flesh into small pieces, rejecting the hard core. Blanch the nuts by pouring boiling water over them and allowing them to stand a few minutes, when the skins can be easily removed. Chop finely and add to the pineapple. Pile in little heaps on lettuce leaves, cover with the dressing and decorate with cherries.

Stuffed Tomato Salad

6 ripe tomatoes.
½ pint cream dressing.
2 cucumbers.

Lettuce.
Salt and pepper.
Parsley.

Scald the tomatoes and remove the skins. Cut a slice from the top of each, and with a small spoon remove the seeds. Peel the cucumbers and cut them into dice, season highly and mix with at least half the dressing. Fill the tomato cups with this and put a spoonful of the dressing on top. Sprinkle a very little finely-chopped parsley over, and serve on a bed of lettuce leaves.

Mayonnaise Dressing

1 egg yolk.	4 tablespoons lemon juice or
½ pint olive oil.	vinegar.
	½ teaspoon salt.
¼ teaspoon paprica or white pepper.	

Break the yolk of the egg into a dry, cold bowl and beat a little. At first add the oil to the egg very slowly (a few drops at a time), and as the dressing begins to thicken, the oil may be added more rapidly till, at the last, a teaspoonful at a time may be stirred in. The dressing must be stirred while the oil is being added, either with a spoon, fork or wire egg beater. Add the vinegar slowly, continuing the beating while it is being mixed. It is better not to add the salt and pepper till the mayonnaise is to be used, because it keeps better if the seasoning is omitted. In any case, even when the dressing is to be used at once, do not add the seasoning till the oil and vinegar, or lemon, are added to the egg.

Tarragon or other flavored vinegars, such as mint or sage, may be substituted in whole or in part for the plain vinegar or lemon juice.

Keep mayonnaise in a cool, dark place.

French Dressing

4 tablespoons olive oil.	¼ teaspoon paprica or
1½ tablespoons vinegar.	pepper.
⅓ teaspoon salt.	1 teaspoon mixed mustard,
	if liked.

Mix the salt and pepper in a shallow dish or saucer; add the mustard, if it is to be used, and pour in the oil. Stir well to mix with the seasonings and add the vinegar, a little at a time, beating the mixture with a fork continuously. Serve as soon as mixed.

Horseradish Dressing

1 cup heavy cream.
1 tablespoon grated or evaporated horseradish.

2 tablespoons lemon juice.
Salt and paprica.

Beat the cream till quite thick and then add the horseradish finely grated. If evaporated horseradish is used, pour over it a tablespoon of cold water and allow it to be absorbed before adding to the whipped cream. Put in the lemon juice slowly, stirring all the time; season to taste, and serve very cold. This dressing is especially good with tomatoes.

Boiled Salad Dressing

2 tablespoons butter.
2 eggs.
1 cup vinegar.

2 teaspoons sugar.
1 teaspoon dry mustard.
⅔ teaspoon salt.
⅓ teaspoon pepper.

Put the butter, sugar, eggs, mustard, salt and pepper into a bowl or the inner part of a double boiler and cook over hot water till they begin to thicken. Add the vinegar and continue the cooking three minutes. Beat the mixture occasionally while cooling. Keep in a cool, dark place. This dressing will remain good several weeks.

Cream Dressing

½ teaspoon salt.
1 teaspoon flour.
2 egg yolks.
¾ cup cream.

1 teaspoon mustard.
1 tablespoon sugar.
2 tablespoons butter.
¼ cup vinegar.

Mix the dry ingredients with the butter; add the yolks of the eggs, then the cream and, lastly, the vinegar, and cook over hot water until it thickens. Strain if necessary, and chill.

Chicken Salad

1 cold cooked fowl.	Mayonnaise dressing.
2 cups celery.	Lettuce.
4 tablespoons oil.	Hard-boiled egg and olives
2 tablespoons vinegar.	for decorating.

Salt and pepper to taste.

After removing all skin and gristle, cut the fowl into dice and mix it with the celery; add the salt and pepper, and marinate for an hour before using with the oil and vinegar. Mix with mayonnaise dressing and garnish with lettuce, hard-boiled egg and stoned olives, or strips of red pepper.

Cocoanut Salad

½ cocoanut, grated.	2 tablespoons onions,
2 apples, pared, cored	chopped.
and chopped.	1 tablespoon parsley,
1 cup celery, chopped.	coarsely chopped.

3 Chili peppers.

Mix, cover with two measures French dressing, chill and serve in lettuce shells or in scooped-out tomatoes.

MEMORANDA

MEMORANDA

EGGS

HARD AND SOFT COOKED EGGS

TO cook eggs so that they will be firm all the way through and yet not tough or indigestible, put them in a saucepan of boiling water, cover closely and place on a part of the stove where the water will remain very hot, but not boil, and let stand for twenty minutes.

To cook eggs so that they will be soft, follow the above directions, but let the eggs remain only ten minutes.

Shirred Eggs

2 eggs.   1 tablespoon butter.
              Salt and pepper to taste.

Melt the butter in an egg shirrer or any fireproof earthen baking-dish; break the eggs into the dish and season to taste. Cook in a moderate oven until set and serve in the baking-dish. Shirred eggs cook very nicely if placed on an asbestos mat on top of the range and covered with another mat kept for such purposes. This saves heating the oven if there is no other baking to be done. A little chopped parsley, cheese or a few fried bread crumbs may be sprinkled over the eggs before cooking, if desired.

Poached or Dropped Eggs

2 eggs.   Boiling salted water.
              Buttered toast.

Have the water boiling in a shallow pan—a frying-pan is good,—salt it lightly and drop in the eggs, one at a time, having previously broken them into a cup to see that they are fresh. Cook till the whites are just set, then lift from the water with a skimmer and place on the hot buttered toast.

An excellent method of insuring the good shape of the eggs is to grease a muffin ring for each egg to be cooked and place in the pan. Drop the egg into the ring which can be easily removed when the cooking is completed.

Scrambled Eggs

6 eggs.	6 tablespoons cream or milk.
2 tablespoons butter.	½ teaspoon salt.
	⅙ teaspoon pepper.

Beat the eggs lightly, whites and yolks together, add the seasoning and cream or milk, and place with the butter in a saucepan. Stir the mixture constantly with a wooden spoon till it begins to thicken, then remove the saucepan to a cooler part of the stove and continue the cooking till the eggs are set. Serve either on buttered toast or garnished with points of toast.

A little grated cheese, a few green peas or mushrooms (cooked), or a few asparagus tips are sometimes added to the scrambled eggs just before removing them from the fire.

Plain Omelet

4 eggs.	¼ teaspoon salt.
4 tablespoons water.	⅛ teaspoon pepper.
	2 tablespoons butter.

Break the eggs into a bowl and beat them lightly, yolks and whites together, add the salt, pepper and water, and mix all well; melt the butter in a clean omelet pan and allow it to become quite hot without browning. Pour the eggs into the pan, mix and stir them gently till they begin to set. Now push the omelet down to one side of the pan that it may be thick and puffy, tilting the pan so as to keep it at one side. Cook till just set in the centre and golden brown on the surface next to the pan. Turn onto a dish, brown side up, and serve plain or with tomato or other sauce.

Orange Omelet

4 eggs.	2 tablespoons butter.
4 tablespoons water.	2 oranges.
¼ teaspoon salt.	Sugar to taste.

Prepare the oranges by removing the skins, every particle of white pith, the seeds and as much as possible of the inner dividing skin; then cut or break into small pieces and add sugar to sweeten. This should be done some time before making the omelet so that the orange juice and sugar may form a syrup.

Separate the whites from the yolks of the eggs; beat first the whites, then the yolks (by beating the whites first the same beater will do for both); add the salt and water to the yolks, then blend with the stiffly-beaten whites. Heat the butter in an omelet pan and when hot, but not browned, pour in the eggs and cook over a moderate, steady heat till the bottom of the omelet is set. This can be ascertained by gently inserting a knife between the omelet and the pan. As soon as set, place the pan on the upper shelf of a fairly hot oven to cook the top. When firm to the touch and slightly browned, remove from the oven and put a few pieces of the orange on the omelet; mark across the centre with a knife, double the two sides together quickly and turn or roll onto a hot dish. Pour the remainder of the orange around it and serve at once, as it soon falls.

Cheese Omelet

3 eggs.	⅛ teaspoon pepper.
3 tablespoons water.	2 tablespoons butter.
2 tablespoons mild grated cheese.	Salt, if needed.

Beat the eggs lightly, yolks and whites together, add the water and seasoning. Melt the butter in an omelet pan, pour in the eggs and stir and mix lightly till they begin to set. Sprinkle the grated cheese over the top, then scrape and push the omelet to one side of the pan. Cook about one minute, then either turn in the pan by slipping a knife under the omelet, or hold the pan for a moment in front of the fire or under the flame of the gas range. Turn onto a hot dish, and serve at once.

Omelet Soufflé

6 eggs.	½ teaspoon any desired
½ cup of sugar.	flavoring.
A pinch of salt.	

Separate the whites and yolks of the eggs and beat the whites to a stiff froth; add the sugar and salt to the yolks and beat till thick. Mix the whites and yolks lightly together and add the flavoring; turn into a buttered soufflé or pudding-dish, and bake in a hot oven from twelve to fourteen minutes.

Serve, as soon as set, in the dish in which it was cooked. Do not keep the soufflé waiting before serving, as it very quickly falls.

Omelet Celestine

Prepare the omelet exactly as for Orange Omelet, omitting the oranges, and in their place spread the omelet, after it is dished, with peach preserve or marmalade, then with finely-chopped, blanched almonds, and cover with whipped cream.

Cheese Soufflé

3 tablespoons flour.	1 cup milk.
3 tablespoons butter.	1 cup grated cheese.
3 eggs. .	Salt and pepper to taste.

Put the butter and flour together in a saucepan and stir till blended without browning. Add the milk, a little at a time, and stir till the mixture boils; then add the grated cheese, salt and pepper, and set aside to cool. Beat the eggs, yolks and whites separately; then add the yolks to the mixture in the saucepan and blend thoroughly. Lastly, fold

in the whites beaten to a stiff froth, and turn the
soufflé into a deep, well-greased dish. Bake in a
moderate oven about twenty-five minutes, and serve
at once as it soon falls.

Chicken Soufflé

1½ tablespoons butter.	½ teaspoon salt.
1½ tablespoons flour.	¼ teaspoon pepper.
1½ cups milk, or milk and	1 cup minced chicken.
chicken stock.	3 eggs.
¼ teaspoon grated lemon	½ cup stale bread crumbs.
rind.	

Blend the butter and flour in a saucepan without
browning; add the milk and stir till boiling; then
put in the salt, pepper, bread crumbs and lemon
rind. Cool, and then stir in the chicken; beat and
add the eggs — the yolks beaten till thick and the
whites till stiff. Bake in a well-greased pan, in a
moderately hot oven, about half an hour.

Lemon Soufflé

¼ cup butter.	3 eggs.
¼ cup flour.	1¼ cups milk.
½ cup sugar.	Grated rind of 1 lemon.
	¼ teaspoon salt.

Put the butter and flour together in a saucepan
and blend smoothly; add the milk, a little at a time,
stirring constantly till boiling; cool, and add the
lemon rind, sugar and salt, then the yolks of the
eggs beaten till thick and, lastly, the whites beaten
to a stiff froth. Turn into a greased pudding-mould
and steam one hour. Serve with a hot sweet sauce.

Swiss Eggs

1 tablespoon butter.	4 eggs.
2 tablespoons grated cheese.	3 tablespoons cream.
4 very thin slices of cheese.	Salt and pepper to taste.

Melt the butter in a shallow baking-dish; cut the
slices of cheese in pieces of convenient size to cover
the bottom of the dish. Break the eggs and drop

them into the dish over the cheese, season to taste, and pour the cream over the eggs; sprinkle the grated cheese on top and bake in a moderate oven till the eggs are set and the cheese a delicate brown.

Eggs in Prison

2 cups of cold, cooked meat.	Stale browned bread crumbs.
4 eggs.	Seasoning and flavoring to suit the meat.

Grease thoroughly four small cups or moulds and sprinkle thickly with the browned crumbs. Season and flavor the meat rather highly, and line the moulds with it, leaving a hollow in the centre of each mould — the meat may be moistened with stock or gravy if too dry, — break a raw egg into the hollow left for the purpose in each cup, sprinkle with salt and pepper, and bake in a moderate oven till the eggs are set. Turn out and serve with or without sauce or gravy.

Japanese Eggs

1½ cups boiled rice.	1 teaspoon onion juice.
6 hard-cooked eggs.	1 teaspoon parsley.
1½ cups white sauce.	1 teaspoon soy or Worcestershire sauce.

Pile the hot, cooked rice on a platter; cut the eggs in quarters and imbed in the rice; pour over them the sauce flavored with the onion juice and the soy or Worcestershire sauce, and sprinkle the chopped parsley over the top.

NOTE. — Soy is a sauce to be found in some stores where Japanese and Chinese products are sold. Its principal ingredient is the soy bean.

Egg Timbales

4 eggs.	Salt and pepper.
2 tablespoons chopped parsley or chopped ham.	4 tablespoons milk or thin cream.
	Tomato or white sauce.

Beat the eggs just enough to thoroughly mix yolks and whites, add the salt, pepper and the milk or cream.

Grease very small cups or moulds and sprinkle the bottoms and sides with the parsley or ham, pour in enough egg to nearly fill each cup and stand in a pan of almost boiling water. Cook either in a moderate oven or over a slow fire, that the water may not boil rapidly and cause the timbales to become "honeycombed." As soon as a knife can be inserted in the timbales and drawn out clean, they are done. Unmould on individual plates, because their delicacy makes them difficult to serve from a platter, and pour the sauce around them.

Savory Eggs

6 eggs.	1 tablespoon vinegar.
2 medium-sized onions.	Salt and paprika to taste.
3 tablespoons butter.	⅓ cup stale bread crumbs.
1 tablespoon grated cheese.	

Heat one and one-half tablespoons of the butter in a frying-pan, and cook in it the onions, which have been peeled and finely minced, till light brown; then turn the onions into a baking-dish that can be sent to the table; spread them over the bottom of the dish and break the eggs over them; add the vinegar and seasoning, and sprinkle with the bread crumbs that have been fried in the remaining tablespoon and a half of butter. Put the cheese over the top and bake in a moderate oven till the eggs are just set.

Curried Eggs

6 hard-cooked eggs.	½ sour apple or a teaspoon
1 very small onion.	of lemon juice.
2 tablespoons butter or	¼ teaspoon salt.
drippings.	1½ cups water, stock or
1 tablespoon flour.	milk.
1 tablespoon curry powder.	

Hard cook the eggs, remove the shells and cut the eggs in slices. Melt the butter or drippings and cook in it the onion, peeled and finely minced; next, put in the flour and curry powder and cook three minutes. Add the stock, water or milk slowly, and stir till the sauce boils; put in the apple or lemon juice and simmer gently for twenty minutes. Add salt, and heat the slices of egg in the hot sauce.

Scotch Eggs

6 hard-cooked eggs.	Salt and pepper to taste.
½ cup stale bread crumbs.	⅔ cup milk.
1 cup minced ham or other meat.	Egg and bread crumbs. Frying fat.

Cook the eggs twenty minutes in water just below the boiling point, stand in cold water for half an hour, then remove the shells and wipe the eggs quite dry.

Cook the half cup of bread crumbs in the milk till thick, add the seasoning and meat and mix all together to form a rather stiff paste. Take a portion of this and press around one of the eggs smoothly with the hand, having the paste of equal thickness all over, and continue till the eggs are covered. Take a raw egg with one tablespoon of water and beat lightly; dip each of the prepared eggs into this and cover every particle with the raw egg. As soon as covered, drop onto a paper containing stale bread crumbs, coat with these and fry in deep fat till golden brown. Cut in halves, stand cut side up, and serve plain or with white or tomato sauce or gravy.

MEMORANDA

MEMORANDA

PUDDINGS AND PUDDING SAUCES

Quince Pudding

2 cups flour.	2 tablespoons melted butter.
2 teaspoons Rumford	1 egg.
Baking Powder.	1½ cups milk.
½ teaspoon salt.	1 cup quince preserve.

Sift together the flour, salt and baking powder; beat the egg, add to it the milk and melted butter, and mix these with the dry ingredients to form a stiff batter. When well mixed, add the preserve and beat well. Turn into a greased baking-pan and bake in a moderate oven about half an hour. Cut in squares, and serve with sweetened whipped cream.

Apricot Soufflé

1 cup canned apricots.	3 egg whites.
½ cup sugar.	6 drops almond extract.

Rub apricots through a sieve; place in saucepan and bring to the boiling point; add the sugar, extract and whites of the eggs beaten to a stiff froth, and mix well with the fruit. Turn into small moulds that have been greased and sprinkled with sugar. Stand in a pan containing enough hot water to come halfway up the sides of the moulds, and bake until firm — about twenty minutes.

Italian Nut Pudding

1 pint milk.	1 tablespoon sherry.
¼ cup sugar.	2 egg yolks.
1 cup macaroni.	⅓ cup nut meats.
½ teaspoon cinnamon.	Whipped cream.

Scald the milk and add to it the macaroni which has been passed through a meat grinder. Cook till the macaroni is tender and the whole of the consistency of a thick custard. Add the sugar and cinnamon, then the sherry, and yolks of the eggs beaten till they are thick. Sprinkle half the nut meats, coarsely chopped, over the bottom of small

93

moulds, fill with the pudding, and put the remainder of the nuts over the top. Stand the moulds in a pan of hot water and bake fifteen minutes. Turn out and serve with whipped cream.

Marmalade Pudding

1 cup stale bread crumbs.	2 eggs.
⅔ cup orange marmalade.	1½ cups milk.
1 teaspoon butter.	

Use the butter to grease a pudding-mould or bowl, then put in the bread crumbs and marmalade in thin layers, till all are used. Beat the eggs lightly, yolks and whites together, and add the milk to form a custard; pour over the ingredients in the bowl and let stand ten minutes. If the pudding-mould has a cover put it on, otherwise cover with a piece of greased paper twisted under the rim of the bowl to keep it in position. Place in a saucepan containing enough boiling water to come two-thirds up the sides of the bowl. Cook one hour, adding more water as that in the pan boils away. Serve hot with a lemon sauce.

Poor Man's Rice Pudding

1 quart milk.	1 tablespoon butter.
2 tablespoons rice.	A pinch of salt.
3 tablespoons sugar.	

Wash the rice well and put it in a baking-dish with the salt, sugar and butter; pour the milk over and bake very slowly, at least two and one-half hours, stirring twice during the first hour.

King George's Pudding

⅓ cup flour.	⅓ cup finely-chopped suet.
1 level cup of any flaked cereal.	1 egg.
⅓ cup sugar.	⅓ cup milk.
½ cup dark-colored jam — plum, raspberry or blackberry.	½ teaspoon salt.
	1 teaspoon Rumford Baking Powder

Put together in a bowl the flour, cereal, sugar, suet, salt and baking powder; beat the egg thor-

oughly and add to it the milk and jam; mix, and use
to moisten the other ingredients. Turn into a well-
greased mould or bowl, cover and steam three hours.
Serve hot with a sweet sauce.

Fig Puffs

1½ cups flour.	2 tablespoons butter.
½ teaspoon salt.	1 egg.
2 teaspoons Rumford Bak-	1¼ cups milk.
ing Powder.	¾ cup chopped figs.

Sift the flour, salt and baking powder, rub in the
butter, then add the figs, mixing them well into the
dry flour. Mix to a stiff batter with the beaten egg
and milk. Bake in small greased pans in a moderately hot oven. Serve hot with a sauce.

Canary Pudding

3 eggs.	Grated rind of 1 lemon.
½ cup butter.	1 teaspoon Rumford Baking
⅔ cup sugar.	Powder.
¾ cup flour.	

Melt the butter, add the sugar, then the flour and
baking powder sifted together; next, the lemon rind,
and lastly, the eggs well beaten. Put into greased
cups and steam three-quarters of an hour. Serve
hot, with or without a sauce.

English Plum Pudding

½ pound suet.	½ teaspoon each ground
¼ pound currants.	cloves, nutmeg and
½ pound seeded raisins.	ginger.
¼ pound sugar.	Grated rind of 2 lemons.
½ pound stale bread	½ pound citron or orange
crumbs.	peel.
¼ pound flour.	6 eggs.
1 teaspoon ground cinnamon.	½ cup brandy.

Chop the suet finely, clean the currants, seed the
raisins, and cut the peel quite small. Put all together into a bowl, add the lemon rind, sugar, spices,
flour and bread crumbs, and moisten with the well-

beaten eggs and brandy. Turn into well-greased bowls or pudding-moulds and steam or boil eight hours. These puddings will keep a year, but need to be boiled for an hour before serving.

Plain Plum Pudding

½ cup finely-chopped beef suet.
½ cup sugar.
1 cup seeded raisins.
½ cup currants.
2 cups flour.

2 teaspoons Rumford Baking Powder.
1 teaspoon mixed spices.
½ teaspoon salt.
¾ cup milk.
1 egg.

Clean the currants and add them to the seeded raisins and suet. Sift the flour with the spices, baking powder and salt and add to the fruit with the sugar; moisten with the egg and milk and turn into a greased pudding-mould. Steam three hours, and serve with hard or lemon sauce.

Date Pudding

½ pound stoned dates.
¼ pound beef suet.
1 cup flour.
½ cup sugar.
1 teaspoon ground ginger.
1 teaspoon ground cinnamon.

1 teaspoon salt.
1 teaspoon Rumford Baking Powder.
1 cup bread crumbs.
2 eggs.
⅔ cup milk.

Chop the dates and suet finely or pass them through a meat chopper; add all the dry ingredients and moisten with the eggs, well beaten, and the milk. Turn into greased moulds, cover and steam — if in one large mould, three hours; if in smaller ones, two hours. Serve hot with hard sauce.

Steamed Orange Pudding

1½ cups scalded milk.
1 cup bread crumbs.
2 tablespoons butter.
3 eggs.

⅓ cup sugar.
The grated rind and strained juice of 2 small oranges.

Pour the scalded milk over the crumbs, add the butter and let the mixture stand for ten minutes;

beat the eggs thoroughly and add them with the sugar; stir in the orange juice and rind, and beat well. Turn into greased moulds, cover, and steam one hour.

Baked Orange Pudding

⅓ cup sugar.
2 tablespoons bread
  crumbs.

The grated rind and strained
  juice of 1 orange.
1 cup milk.
1 egg.

Beat the egg thoroughly and add the orange and sugar; scald the milk and pour it over the crumbs; add the first mixture and, when well mixed, pour into a baking-dish. Bake till set like a custard, and serve cold.

Mother Eve's Pudding

4 eggs.
4 apples.
1½ cups bread crumbs.

¾ cup sugar.
Pinch of salt.
Slight grating of nutmeg.

Peel, core and chop the apples finely; add the bread crumbs, sugar, salt and nutmeg. Beat the eggs well and use them to moisten the pudding. Turn into a greased mould, cover closely and steam two hours. Serve with a hot sweet sauce.

Apple Puffs

1 cup flour.
½ cup sugar.
3 apples.
1 egg.

1 teaspoon Rumford Baking
  Powder.
1 cup milk.
Pinch of salt.

Sift together the flour, salt and baking powder; add the sugar and the apples peeled, cored and chopped; mix to a rather stiff batter with the egg and milk. Drop by spoonfuls into hot fat and cook till the puffs are golden brown and the apples tender. Drain on soft paper, and serve hot with a sauce.

Cherry Pudding

1 pound stoned cherries.	1 cup milk.
½ cup sugar.	4 tablespoons flour.
3 eggs.	A pinch of salt.

Grease a pudding-mould or bowl and put in it the cherries that have been stoned, and mixed with the sugar. Make a batter by beating the eggs and adding them to the flour which has been sifted with the salt; mix in the milk and beat to remove all lumps. Pour this batter over the cherries; cover the mould, and steam the pudding one and one-half hours.

Lemon Snowballs

3 eggs.	2 tablespoons lemon juice.
1 cup granulated sugar.	1 cup flour.
3 tablespoons water.	1 teaspoon Rumford Baking
The grated rind of 1 lemon.	Powder.

Beat the yolk of the eggs and sugar together till very light, add the water, lemon juice and rind; then the flour and baking powder sifted together. Beat the whites of the eggs till stiff, add them to the batter and fold in as gently as possible. Grease small cups, put a heaping tablespoon of the batter in each, and steam or boil for half an hour. Turn out, roll in powdered sugar, and serve with a lemon sauce.

Brown Betty

2 cups fine bread crumbs.	3 cups stewed sweetened apples.
3 tablespoons butter.	

Melt the butter and add the crumbs, stirring till they have absorbed it all. Grease a pudding-dish, put a layer of the buttered crumbs in the bottom, then a layer of apples, then more crumbs and so on, till the dish is full or the ingredients all used. Have crumbs for the top layer and sprinkle a few bits of butter over them. Bake in a moderate oven three-quarters of an hour.

Cottage Pudding

2 cups flour.
2 teaspoons Rumford Baking Powder.
⅓ teaspoon salt.

¼ cup sugar.
1 egg.
2 tablespoons melted butter.
1 cup milk.

Sift together the flour, salt and baking powder; add the sugar and mix to a stiff batter with the egg, butter and milk. Bake in a shallow, greased dish about half an hour. Serve hot with sauce.

Rice Cream

1 quart milk.
½ cup rice.
3 tablespoons sugar.

1 rounding tablespoon granulated gelatine.
½ pint whipped cream.

Scald the milk in a double boiler, add the rice and cook till tender. Turn out, add the sugar and, when nearly cold, add the gelatine which has been dissolved by standing in half a cup of milk for ten minutes; then heat both milk and gelatine till the latter is melted. As soon as the mixture shows signs of setting, add the whipped cream, stir it in lightly, and turn into a wet mould. Chill thoroughly, turn out, and serve with fresh or cooked fruit.

Bavarian Cream

1 pint milk or half milk and half thin cream.
3 eggs.

⅓ cup cold water.
⅔ cup sugar.
½ pint whipped cream.
1 tablespoon granulated gelatine.

Soak the gelatine in the cold water. Cook the yolks of the eggs and milk (or milk and cream) in a double boiler, stirring constantly till they coat the back of the spoon; add the sugar and soaked gelatine. Let the mixture become almost cold, then add the whipped cream and the stiffly-beaten whites of the eggs, which blend thoroughly with the other ingredients, and turn into a wet mould. When chilled, serve with custard, cream or fruit.

Peach Cream

1 quart peaches.	1 cup whipped cream.
1 cup water.	1 tablespoon granulated
⅔ cup sugar.	gelatine.
	¼ cup cold water.

Cook the peaches till tender with the water and sugar, then pass them through a sieve. Soak the gelatine for ten minutes in the quarter cup of cold water, then heat it to the boiling point and add to the peaches. Whip the cream stiffly and add to the fruit pulp when the latter is nearly cold; mix smoothly and turn into a china or granite mould. Have the cream very cold when turned out. The mould may be decorated with sections of fresh peaches if desired. Canned peaches can be used for making this dessert.

Coffee Cream

1½ cups milk.	1 tablespoon granulated
3 eggs.	gelatine.
½ cup sugar.	⅔ cup strong coffee.
	1 cup whipped cream.

Make a custard by cooking the eggs and milk in a double boiler till they coat the back of a spoon, stirring while the mixture is cooking; soak the gelatine for ten minutes in the coffee, and add to the custard, which should be hot enough to dissolve the gelatine. Put in the sugar and stand the mixture aside to cool while the cream is being whipped; add the cream when the first mixture is nearly cold, stir in thoroughly and turn into a wet mould. Chill before serving.

Cold Wine Sauce

1 cup sugar.	½ cup claret.
1 cup water.	Juice of 1 lemon.

Boil the sugar and water together till they form a thick syrup. Let the syrup cool, add the wine and lemon juice, and let the sauce become thoroughly cold before serving.

Maple Sauce

2 egg yolks.   ½ cup whipped cream.
⅔ cup hot maple syrup.   Pinch of salt.

Beat the yolks of the eggs well and pour the hot syrup over them. Cook in a double boiler till of the consistency of thin custard. When cold add the salt and whipped cream, and serve at once.

Wine Sauce

3 tablespoons butter.   1 cup fine sugar.
              3 tablespoons sherry.

Beat the butter and sugar till light, put the bowl containing them over hot water and stir till the contents are creamy, and then add the wine. Serve at once.

Cranberry Sauce

1 quart cranberries.   1½ cups water.
              2 cups sugar.

Cook the cranberries and water till the berries are tender; then rub through a sieve to keep back the skins and seeds. Return to the fire, add the sugar and cook only until it is melted. Chill and serve.

Foamy Sauce

3 tablespoons apricot,   1 cup boiling water.
    marmalade or peach   1 tablespoon cornstarch.
    preserve.   2 tablespoons cold water.
Juice of 1 lemon.   1 egg white.
              Sugar if required.

Put the preserve, lemon juice and water into a saucepan and bring to the boiling point, adding a little sugar if it is needed, and stir in the cornstarch moistened with the cold water. Cook five minutes and pour over the stiffly-beaten white of egg, stirring constantly while this is being done. Serve at once.

Hot Chocolate Sauce

2 squares of chocolate.	1 cup milk.
½ cup sugar.	2 egg yolks.

An inch stick of cinnamon or any other flavoring desired.

Melt the chocolate in the upper vessel of a double boiler, add the milk a little at a time, and cook with the sugar and cinnamon over hot water. When scalding hot add the yolks of eggs well beaten, and stir till the sauce thickens. Remove the cinnamon before serving.

Hard Sauce

½ cup butter.	2 tablespoons boiling water.
1 cup powdered sugar.	Flavoring to taste.

Beat the butter in a bowl till creamy, then add half of the sugar and water; beat well, and add the remainder of the sugar and water. When light and fluffy add the flavoring and set aside in a cool place till wanted. If desired the flavoring may be omitted and a little nutmeg grated over the sauce in the serving dish.

NOTE. — The addition of the water makes the sauce lighter and lessens the labor of beating.

Chocolate Sauce (without egg)

½ cup sugar.	½ cup milk.
1 cup water.	1 tablespoon cornstarch.
3 tablespoons grated chocolate.	1 inch stick cinnamon.

Boil the sugar and water together to a syrup, pour this over the chocolate and return to the saucepan with the cinnamon, and cook ten minutes. Moisten the cornstarch with the milk, stir into the boiling syrup, and cook five minutes longer. Remove the cinnamon before serving.

MEMORANDA

MEMORANDA

PASTRY

IN making pastry the best results are obtained by having all the ingredients as cold as possible, and keeping them so till the pastry goes into the oven. It is the sudden change in temperature, as much as the actual ingredients used, that makes pastry light. If soft butter and lukewarm water are used the result must be poor pastry—tough and not appetizing.

For plain paste, lard or a mixture of lard and butter should be used; for very plain crusts, lard and good beef drippings; but for puff paste, butter must be used.

It is often desirable to have pastry that is light, flaky and tender without being too rich, and this result can be attained by the addition of a little Rumford Baking Powder and the reduction of the amount of fat used. *Where a rule calls for one and one-half cups of flour and two-thirds of a cup of fat — lard or butter — the housekeeper may take half a cup of fat and a teaspoonful of Rumford Baking Powder to the cup and a half of flour, and have equally good results as to appearance and flavor, at much less expense.*

All paste is better if chilled before it is baked. If convenient it should be made the day before it is to be used.

In making fruit pies always put the sugar with the fruit — not on top — or the crust will be soggy.

A marble or slate pastry-board and a glass or china rolling-pin are the best for pastry, because of their coldness; but if the ordinary utensils are cold, good results will be obtained.

Short Paste

3 cups flour.
1 teaspoon salt.
1 teaspoon Rumford Baking Powder.

1 cup lard, or lard and butter.
Ice-cold water to mix — about 1½ cups.

Sift together the flour, salt and baking powder; rub in lightly with the fingers the lard and butter,

105

mix to a firm dough with the ice-cold water and roll
out once on a floured board.   Use for whatever purpose desired.

Five-minute Paste

2 cups flour.	¾ cup butter.
½ teaspoon salt.	1 egg yolk.
½ teaspoon Rumford Bak-	Ice-cold water.
ing Powder.	

Sift together the flour, salt and baking powder; then
cream the butter in a bowl as for a cake.   As soon as
it is light and creamy, add the sifted flour, mixing it in
with a knife, not touching at all with the hands.   Beat
the yolk of egg and add a little ice water to it —
probably about three-quarters of a cup will be required
— to moisten the paste.   Roll out once on a floured
board.   The egg may be omitted, but is an improvement
if used.

Flaky Paste

3 cups flour.	1⅓ cups lard, or butter and
1 teaspoon salt.	lard.
Ice-cold water to mix.	

Sift the flour and salt together into a bowl, chop in
the shortening with a knife till well mixed with the
flour.   Add ice-cold water to form a dough, cutting and
mixing the paste thoroughly while adding the water.
Flour a board and roll the paste out thinly, rolling
only lengthwise, and keeping the edges straight; then
fold evenly into three layers (lengthwise as a sheet of
paper would be folded to fit a business envelope), turn
it half around and roll again.   Repeat the folding and
rolling twice, and chill the paste if possible before
baking.   It is the folding and rolling that produce the
flakes.

Puff Paste

½ pound pastry flour.	1 teaspoon salt.
½ pound butter.	1 egg yolk.
1 tablespoon lemon juice.	Ice-cold water.

Beat the egg and add to it the water and lemon
juice; sift flour and salt, and mix all these ingredients
to a firm dough.   Roll out into an oblong sheet.
Wash the butter and press into a flat cake half as

large as the dough, lay it on one end and cover with the paste, like a fruit turnover. Press the edges well together, roll out and fold into three layers. Cool and roll again, repeating the process till the paste has been rolled seven times. Put on ice when necessary. Bake in a hot oven, and if possible make it the day before it is required for use. The butter may be divided into three portions and put in after each rolling if desired, but the seven rollings must be made after all the butter has been used.

Apple Custard Pie

3 large tart apples.   ½ pint milk.
½ cup sugar.   Nutmeg or cinnamon to taste.
2 eggs.   Paste.

Peel, core and stew the apples with just enough water to prevent burning, rub through a sieve, and add the sugar and spice. Beat the eggs — yolks and whites separately, — add the yolks to the milk, stir in the flavored apples, and fold into the mixture the stiffly-beaten whites of the eggs. Line a deep pie plate with paste, pour in the filling, and put strips of paste lattice-fashion over the top. Bake in a moderate oven about half an hour.

Mince Pie Filling

1 pound seeded raisins.   1 pound sugar.
1 pound currants.   2 pounds peeled, cored and
1 pound finely-chopped   chopped apples.
   beef suet.   1¼ teaspoons mixed spices.
The grated rind of 2   1 cup brandy.
   lemons.   1 tablespoon salt.
½ pound candied orange peel and citron chopped fine.

Prepare the fruits by seeding the raisins, washing and drying both these and the currants; add the suet very finely chopped. Run the peel through a meat chopper or chop it very fine with a knife, and mix all together with the sugar, spices, grated lemon rind, apples, salt and brandy. Keep at least a week before using, stirring occasionally. This quantity will make about eight good-sized pies, and will keep all winter.

Cranberry and Raisin Pie

1½ cups cranberries.   ½ cup sugar.
1 cup raisins.   Paste.

Seed the raisins and chop the cranberries; add the
sugar, and bake in a shallow pie plate between two
crusts.

Pumpkin Pie

2 cups steamed or baked   1 teaspoon cinnamon.
    pumpkin.   1 teaspoon ginger.
1 cup sugar.   1 pint scalded milk.
½ teaspoon salt.   2 large eggs.
               Paste.

Rub the pumpkin through a sieve and add to it
the sugar, salt, spices, milk and well-beaten eggs.
Cool and use to fill a large pie plate which has been
lined with paste. Bake in a moderate oven about forty
minutes.

Lemon Meringue Pie

1 cup water.   The juice and grated rind
1 cup sugar.   of 1 lemon.
2 heaping teaspoons corn-   A pinch of salt.
    starch.   2 tablespoons sugar for
2 eggs.   the meringue.
               Paste.

Boil the water and sugar together, add the cornstarch moistened with a little cold water, and cook
five minutes. Then put in the yolks of the eggs, the
lemon juice, rind and salt. Cool slightly and pour
into a previously baked crust. Cover with a meringue
made by beating the whites of the eggs with the two
tablespoons of sugar. Put into a moderately warm
oven to set and brown the meringue.

The reason so many meringues are failures is because they are baked in too hot an oven and consequently browned before the white of the egg has had
time to set all the way through.

Orange Cream Pie

3 eggs.   Grated rind of 2 oranges and
1 cup sugar.   juice of 1.
2 tablespoons cornstarch.   1½ cups milk.
               Paste.

Separate the whites from the yolks of the eggs and beat the yolks, with half the sugar, till light. Mix the cornstarch smoothly with one-fourth cup of the milk, and scald the remainder in a double boiler. When almost boiling, stir in the cornstarch and cook till thick; add the yolks of the eggs, sugar, orange rind and juice; cool slightly and pour into a previously baked crust. Beat the whites of the eggs stiffly, add the remainder of the sugar, and flavor, if liked, with a little orange juice or grated rind. Pile on top of the pie, and put in a moderate oven to set and brown slightly.

Cheese Tartlets

2 tablespoons butter.
½ cup bread crumbs.
2 small eggs.
½ cup grated cheese.

1 teaspoon Rumford Baking Powder.
⅓ cup milk.
Paste.

Beat the butter to a cream, add the bread crumbs alternately with the well-beaten eggs, stir in the cheese, and then add the milk and baking powder. Line small tins with paste and put a tablespoonful of the cheese mixture in each. Bake in a moderate oven about fifteen minutes. Serve hot or cold.

Cheese Cakes

1¼ cups cottage cheese.
½ cup sugar.
3 eggs.

3 tablespoons cream.
Grated rind of 1 lemon.
Paste.

Mix together the cheese, sugar, cream and lemon rind; then add the eggs, yolks and whites well beaten together. Line small tins with paste and nearly fill them with the cheese-cake mixture. Bake in a moderate oven about fifteen minutes.

English Fruit Tart

Fresh fruit.
Short or Flaky paste.

Sugar to taste.

Prepare the fruit and place with the sugar in a deep baking-dish. Add a little water to make juice, the quantity depending on the fruit used. Roll the crust thinly and cover the fruit with it, wetting the edge of the dish to make the crust adhere. Bake in a moderate oven about half an hour. Serve hot or cold and with or without cream or custard.

Any fresh fruit, such as apples, plums, currants, etc., may be used.

Lemon Cheese Cakes

⅓ cup butter.
½ cup sugar.
Grated rind and strained juice of 2 lemons.

2 large eggs.
Puff paste patty shells, previously baked.

Put the butter, sugar, lemon juice and rind in the inner vessel of a double boiler and heat over hot water. When thoroughly heated, add the eggs well beaten, and stir till the mixture thickens. Set aside to become thoroughly cold and then place a spoonful in each patty shell The lemon cheese mixture will keep for months.

Puff Paste Patties.

Roll puff paste very thinly and cut into rounds, or any other shape preferred. With a cutter several sizes smaller remove the centres from half the portions first cut; place the rings thus formed on the whole portions of paste, first wetting the edges of these that the rings may adhere. Chill thoroughly before baking.

Suet Crust for Boiled Puddings

3 cups flour.
1 teaspoon salt.
1 teaspoon Rumford Baking Powder.

1 cup beef suet, free from skin.
Ice-cold water.

Sift together the flour, salt and baking powder; add the finely-chopped suet, and mix to a firm dough with the water; roll out thinly and use to line a well-greased bowl. Fill with fruit sweetened to taste, adding a little water to make a juice. Cover with more crust and tie a floured cloth over the top. Steam or boil at least two and a half hours.

For a meat pudding substitute uncooked meat, well seasoned, cut in small pieces. With a meat pudding a little hole may be cut in the top crust after the pudding is turned out for serving and a cup of boiling water poured in to form additional gravy.

Rumford Dumplings

1½ cups flour.
⅓ teaspoon salt.
1½ teaspoons Rumford Baking Powder.

About ⅔ cup milk (enough to make of the consistency of biscuit dough).

Sift together flour, salt and baking powder; add milk, and then pat or roll on a board till half an inch thick. Cut out with a very small cutter and drop into the boiling stew. Cook ten minutes without removing the lid of the saucepan. If the lid is lifted before the dough is cooked the rush of cold air may cause the dumplings to fall.

Boiled Fruit Dumplings

Make a dough by the rule previously given for Rumford Dumplings, roll as directed, and cut into squares of about three inches. Put a spoonful of berries, plums or a small pared and cored apple in the centre of the dough with sugar to taste. Wet and press the edges of the dough firmly over the fruit so that they will cling together. Tie each dumpling in a square of cheese cloth and plunge into fast boiling water. Cook from half to three-quarters of an hour, according to the fruit used. Serve with a hard or liquid sauce.

For baked apple or other fruit dumplings inclose the fruit in a square of either short or flaky paste (see pages 105 and 106), press the edges firmly together and bake in a moderately hot oven about twenty minutes to half an hour, according to the fruit used. Serve hot with a hard or liquid sauce.

Egg Dumplings

1 egg.
3 tablespoons milk.
⅔ cup flour.

1 teaspoon Rumford Baking Powder.
¼ teaspoon salt.

Beat the egg till light, add the milk and mix. Sift together flour, salt and baking powder, and add the egg and milk to these to form a heavy batter, using a little more milk if necessary. Drop by spoonfuls into hot gravy, and cook fifteen minutes without removing the lid from the saucepan.

Lobster Patties

(10 patties)

1 cup cream sauce.	1 teaspoon lemon juice.
1 cup lobster meat.	Salt and pepper to taste.
A slight grating of nutmeg.	1 egg yolk.
	Puff paste patty shells.

Make the cream sauce by blending in a saucepan two tablespoons of butter with the same quantity of flour; then, when smooth, add half a cup each of milk and thin cream. Stir till boiling, cook five minutes and then put in the seasonings, and lobster cut into dice.

Heat thoroughly and, just before serving, add the yolk of the egg. Fill the shells and serve.

Oyster Patties

(10 patties)

3 tablespoons butter.	1 teaspoon lemon juice.
2 tablespoons flour.	Salt and pepper or cayenne.
½ cup cream.	1 cup solid oysters.
½ cup oyster liquor.	Puff paste patty shells.

Blend the butter and flour in a saucepan, add the cream and oyster liquor, stir till boiling and cook slowly five minutes longer. Pick over the oysters, free them from all bits of shell, scald them in their own liquor (if very large divide them), and add to the hot sauce, together with the seasonings. Bring almost to the boiling point, and fill the shells. Serve hot.

Chicken Patties

Prepare these the same as Oyster Patties, substituting chicken liquor for oyster liquor, and diced chicken for the oysters. A little grated lemon rind may also be substituted for the lemon juice.

MEMORANDA

MEMORANDA

BREAD, ROLLS, MUFFINS, ETC.

IN making breads raised with baking powder always
sift the powder with the dry ingredients to insure
thorough incorporation and perfect mixing. In
making baking powder biscuits, always add enough
liquid to make a very soft dough, as this is one of
the first requirements for good biscuits. Have the
liquid cold, and mix with a flexible knife in preference to handling it with either a spoon or the hand,
because the steel blade is cold, and cuts and mixes
more thoroughly. The less biscuits are handled, the
better. If placed a little apart in the pan they will
be lighter and more crusty.

Always add liquid to dry ingredients — they will
mix more smoothly. The smaller the biscuits and
muffins, the hotter may be the oven. To obtain a
brown crust, brush over with milk before baking.
For a tender crust, brush with melted butter.

Gems and muffins will be lighter and crisper if
baked in pans that are hissing hot before the batter
is placed in them.

Rumford Biscuit

1 quart flour.	2 tablespoons butter or lard.
1 teaspoon salt.	Milk or milk and water to
2 rounding teaspoons Rumford	mix (about 1½ to
Baking Powder.	2 cups).

Sift well together the flour, salt and baking powder; rub in the fat as lightly as possible with the
fingers, just working it until the fat is well blended
with the flour. Then mix to a very soft dough with
the milk, or milk and water, having this always as
cold as possible. Mix with a flexible knife in preference to either a spoon or the hand, as the steel blade
of the knife is colder than the spoon, and also because
it cuts and mixes the dough more thoroughly. Turn
the dough onto a well-floured board, and roll or pat
it with the hand until about three-quarters of an

115

inch thick. Cut into biscuit and lay them, not touching each other, on a baking-pan. Bake in a quick oven twelve or fourteen minutes.

The chief requirements for good biscuit are: 1. *A very soft dough, so soft as to be almost sticky;* 2. *Very little handling, because much manipulation destroys their lightness;* 3. *A very quick oven. If biscuit are not allowed to touch each other in the pan, they will be lighter and more delicate than when placed close together.*

Whole Wheat Biscuit

2 cups whole wheat flour.	1 small egg.
2 teaspoons Rumford Baking Powder.	½ teaspoon salt.
	2 tablespoons butter or lard.
About 1 cup milk.	

Sift together the flour, salt and baking powder; rub in the butter or lard and mix to a light dough with the egg and milk. Roll out on a floured board, cut into biscuits and bake about fifteen minutes in a hot oven.

Rye Biscuit

2 cups rye flour.	2 tablespoons butter.
½ teaspoon salt.	1 small egg.
2 teaspoons Rumford Baking Powder.	About 1 cup milk.

Sift together flour, salt and baking powder; rub in the butter and mix to a light dough with the egg and milk. Roll out on a floured board, cut into biscuits and bake about fifteen minutes in a hot oven.

Potato Biscuit

2 good-sized potatoes.	½ teaspoon salt.
3 cups flour.	¼ cup butter or lard.
3 teaspoons Rumford Baking Powder.	1 egg.
	About 1 cup milk.

Boil and mash the potatoes, having them free from lumps. Sift the flour, salt and baking powder;

add the potatoes and rub in the butter or lard. Mix to a light dough with the egg and milk, roll out a little thinner than ordinary biscuit, and bake in a hot oven. Serve as soon as done.

Maple Rolls

1½ cups flour.
1½ teaspoons Rumford Baking Powder.
½ teaspoon salt.
2 tablespoons butter.
About ½ cup milk.
Scraped maple sugar.

Sift together the flour, salt and baking powder; rub in the butter the same as for Rumford Biscuit and, when well mixed, add the milk, using enough to make a soft dough. Roll this out on a floured board, about one-third inch thick, spread thickly with the scraped maple sugar, roll up like a jelly roll and cut into slices with a very sharp knife. Lay these on a greased baking-pan and bake from twelve to fifteen minutes.

Parker House Rolls

2 cups flour.
2 teaspoons Rumford Baking Powder.
2 teaspoons sugar.
½ teaspoon salt.
2 tablespoons butter.
⅜ cup milk.

Mix as for Rumford Biscuit. Roll to one-third inch in thickness, cut with a round or oval cutter, and crease in the centre with the handle of a case-knife first dipped in flour. Brush one-half with melted butter and fold over. Put in a pan, one-half inch apart, and bake in a quick oven fifteen minutes.

Quick Graham Rolls

2 cups Graham flour.
1 cup white flour.
½ teaspoon salt.
2 rounding teaspoons Rumford Baking Powder.
2 tablespoons butter or lard.
About 1½ cups milk.

Sift together the flour, salt and baking powder; rub in the fat and mix to a smooth dough with the milk. Flour a board well, turn out the dough, divide it into small portions and form into rolls the size and thickness of two fingers. Bake on a flat, greased pan, brushing the rolls over with softened butter before baking.

French Rolls

1 pint milk.	3 pints flour.
2 eggs.	3 tablespoons butter.
1 teaspoon salt.	1 yeast cake.
	2 teaspoons sugar.

Have the milk lukewarm; add to it the well-beaten eggs and salt. Sift the flour and rub the butter into it; mix the yeast and sugar together, working them with the back of a teaspoon until the yeast liquifies, then pour it into the milk and egg and add all these to the flour. Knead to a dough as for bread; let it rise three hours, having the dough covered that a crust may not form on the top, and keep it in a warm room free from draughts. Form into rolls and let these rise again about half an hour, or until they are very light. The length of time will depend somewhat on the temperature of the room.

Bake the rolls in a quick oven, brushing over with butter before baking to brown them more.

Larchmont Muffins

2 cups flour.	1 tablespoon sugar.
½ teaspoon salt.	1 tablespoon melted butter.
2 teaspoons Rumford Baking Powder.	2 eggs.
	1 cup milk.

Sift together the flour, salt and baking powder; add the sugar, then the beaten yolks of eggs, milk and melted butter. Beat thoroughly and fold in gently the stiffly-beaten whites of the eggs. Half fill greased pans and bake about twenty minutes in a moderately hot oven.

Cream Muffins

1½ cups flour.   2 eggs.
⅓ teaspoon salt.   ¼ cup melted butter.
1½ teaspoons Rumford Bak-   ⅔ cup thin cream.
  ing Powder.

Sift together the flour, salt and baking powder;
add the yolks of the eggs, melted butter and cream,
and beat well.   Last of all fold in the stiffly-beaten
whites of the eggs and bake in greased muffin pans in
a moderate oven about twenty minutes.

Graham Gems

3 cups Graham flour.   2 eggs.
½ teaspoon salt.   3 cups milk.
2 rounding teaspoons Rumford   2 tablespoons melted butter.
  Baking Powder.

Sift together the flour, salt and baking powder;
beat the eggs well and add them with the milk and
butter to form a batter.   Bake in hot, greased gem
pans in a moderately hot oven about twenty minutes.

Date Gems

1 cup chopped dates.   ⅓ cup butter.
2 cups flour.   1 egg.
½ teaspoon salt.   1½ cups milk.
          2 teaspoons Rumford Baking Powder.

Stone the dates and chop coarsely.   Sift together
the flour, salt and baking powder.   Rub the butter
into the flour, then mix in the dates and form to a
stiff batter with the beaten egg and milk.   Bake in
hot, well-greased gem pans in a moderate oven
about twenty minutes.

Pop-Overs

1 cup sifted flour.   ⅓ teaspoon salt.
1 cup milk.   2 eggs.

Sift together the flour and salt; add the eggs
well beaten, also the milk.   Beat hard with a Dover

beater for two minutes, then pour at once into hissing hot, greased gem pans, and bake about twenty-five minutes in a hot oven.

Quick Breakfast Puffs

2 eggs.   1½ cups flour.
1 cup milk.   2 teaspoons Rumford Baking
1 tablespoon melted butter.   Powder.
                  ½ teaspoon salt.

Beat the eggs very thoroughly and add the milk and butter. Sift the flour, salt and baking powder twice; add the liquid ingredients, and beat two minutes. Pour into hot, well-greased muffin pans and bake twenty minutes in a hot oven.

Oatmeal Sticks

3 cups flour.   ¼ cup butter.
½ teaspoon salt.   1½ cups scalded milk.
1 tablespoon sugar.   ½ cup oatmeal or rolled oats.
           3 teaspoons Rumford Baking Powder.

Sift together the flour, salt, sugar and baking powder; rub in the butter, scald the milk and pour it over the oatmeal; cool, mix with the other ingredients, and work with the hands till smooth; then roll into sticks about the length and thickness of a lead pencil. Bake about ten minutes in a rather hot oven.

Hot Cross Buns

1½ cups milk.   ⅔ cup currants and raisins
¼ cup butter.   mixed.
½ teaspoon cinnamon.   ⅓ cup sugar.
1 quart flour.   ½ yeast cake.
⅓ teaspoon salt.   1 egg.
           1 teaspoon sugar (for yeast).

Scald the milk with the butter and sugar and allow the mixture to cool till lukewarm. Work the yeast, with the teaspoon of sugar, till it liquifies, and add it to the milk; add also the egg lightly beaten. Put in the currants and raisins, then sift and add the flour, salt and cinnamon. Knead to a dough the same as for bread, and let it rise in a warm place free from draughts till very light. Divide into portions a little larger than biscuits, work till smooth, roll into rounds and place on a greased baking-pan, a little distance apart. Let them rise once more till light, then bake in a moderate oven. Just before baking mark a cross on top of each bun. When nearly done brush over with milk or white of egg, sprinkle with sugar and return to the oven for a moment.

Rumford Whole Wheat Bread

3 cups fine whole wheat flour.
3 teaspoons Rumford Baking Powder.
1 teaspoon salt.

Milk or milk and water to mix to a light, soft dough (about 1¼ cups).
2 teaspoons sugar if desired.

Sift together twice the dry ingredients; place in a large bowl and mix to a dough with the milk or milk and water, mixing with either a spoon or knife. When smooth turn into a greased pan and cover with another pan inverted, unless the double round sandwich pan is used, in which case fill the lower section of pan. Let the bread stand five or ten minutes, then bake in a steady oven, not too hot, about forty-five minutes.

Rumford Dyspeptic Bread

1 pint flour.
1 teaspoon salt.
Milk and water to mix.

2 rounding teaspoons Rumford Baking Powder.

Sift together the flour, salt and baking powder, and mix to a soft dough with the milk and water. Knead two minutes, turn into a greased pan and

allow the bread to rise ten minutes before baking.
Bake slowly for forty minutes.

*This bread can be eaten by those with weak digestion
who can not assimilate bread prepared with yeast.*

Southern Egg Bread

1 pint white corn meal.	3 eggs.
1 teaspoon salt.	1 tablespoon melted butter.
2 teaspoons Rumford Bak-	1½ cups milk.
ing Powder.	1 cup cold boiled rice.

Sift together the corn meal, salt and baking powder; add the eggs well beaten, then the melted
butter, milk and rice. Beat thoroughly, pour into
a shallow, well-greased pan and bake half an hour
in a hot oven.

Corn Bread

2 eggs.	3 heaping tablespoons flour.
½ teaspoon salt.	Yellow corn meal to form a
2 cups milk.	batter.
3 tablespoons sugar.	2 heaping teaspoons Rumford
	Baking Powder.

Beat the eggs well, add the salt, milk and sugar,
and beat in the flour and baking powder with enough
corn meal to form a soft batter; bake in shallow,
well-greased pans in a moderate oven about half an
hour. The exact quantity of corn meal can not be
given — usually about two cups will be sufficient.

Baked Brown Bread

2 cups Graham flour.	1 level teaspoon soda.
1 cup white flour.	½ cup sugar.
½ teaspoon salt.	1 pint sour milk.

Sift the flour, salt and soda twice; add the sugar
and mix to a batter with the milk. Pour into a
well-greased pan and bake in a slow oven about forty
minutes.

Steamed Brown Bread

2 cups Graham flour.   ½ teaspoon salt.
1 cup yellow corn meal.   ½ cup molasses.
2 teaspoons Rumford Bak-   ½ cup raisins.
    ing Powder.   1 egg.
              2 cups sweet milk.

Sift together the flour, corn meal, salt and baking powder; add the raisins and molasses, and mix with the beaten egg and milk.

Have ready well-greased tins with tightly fitting lids, fill two-thirds full of the batter; grease and fit on the covers, and steam three hours. The loaves may be placed in the oven for a few minutes after steaming, if a dry crust is desired.

Yeast Bread

½ cake compressed yeast.   1 teaspoon salt.
1 teaspoon sugar.   Lukewarm water or milk
3 pints sifted flour.   and water to mix (about
1 tablespoon lard or butter   2½ cups).

Work the yeast and sugar together with the back of a teaspoon till they become liquid; add three-fourths cup of lukewarm water and a teaspoon of flour, and stand aside in a warm place while the flour is prepared.

Sift the flour and salt together into a large bowl and rub in the shortening. Make a hollow in the centre of the flour, pour in the yeast and add nearly the remainder of the lukewarm liquid; knead till a soft, elastic dough is formed, using the remainder of the liquid if required. The exact quantity of liquid can not be given, this depending on the quality of the flour. Knead steadily and quickly for twenty minutes, working in all the dry flour and adding a little more if the dough sticks to the bowl or the hands, but avoid adding more than is absolutely necessary.

Cover the dough with a cloth, stand in a moderately warm place free from draughts, and let it rise till it has doubled its bulk. In the daytime, in a warm kitchen, this will probably be about four hours; at night, when the temperature is lower, the bread will be ready to mould into loaves early in the morning. Should it have risen fully before the cook is ready to attend to it, the dough may be "cut down" from the sides of the bowl and allowed to come up again. This will prevent over-raising, and consequent souring.

In forming into loaves, turn the dough onto a lightly-floured board, divide into portions, knead slightly and put into greased pans; cover with a cloth and allow the dough to double its bulk.

In baking bread have the oven only moderately hot when the bread first goes in so as to allow it to rise to its fullest extent; then increase the heat to form a good crust, and, finally, reduce it again to let the centre of the loaf cook thoroughly. Loaves this size require about three-quarters of an hour to bake and when done must be removed at once from the pans and put where the air will circulate freely around them till cold.

MEMORANDA

MEMORANDA

WAFFLES, GRIDDLE CAKES, ETC.

Rumford Waffles

1 cup flour.	2 eggs.
½ teaspoon salt.	1 cup milk.
2 teaspoons Rumford Baking Powder.	2 tablespoons melted butter.

Sift together the flour, salt and baking powder; add the yolks of the eggs and milk, beating well so as to make a smooth batter. Stir in the melted butter and, at the last moment, put in the stiffly-beaten whites of the eggs. Bake in hot, well-greased waffle irons, turning the cakes just as soon as possible after the batter is put in all the compartments of the iron.

Corn Meal Waffles

¼ cup corn meal.	1 teaspoon salt.
1½ cups boiling water.	2 teaspoons Rumford Baking Powder.
1 cup milk.	
¾ cup flour.	¼ cup sugar.
	2 eggs.

Cook the corn meal in the boiling water till quite soft; add the salt and milk and set aside to cool. Sift together flour, sugar and baking powder; add the well-beaten eggs, then the corn meal mixture, with more milk if necessary to make the batter thin enough to pour. Bake in hot, well-greased waffle irons, and serve as soon as cooked.

Cereal Waffles

1 cup cold, cooked oatmeal or other cereal.	2 eggs.
	1 cup milk.
1 cup Graham or entire wheat flour.	2 teaspoons Rumford Baking Powder.
½ teaspoon salt.	

Sift together the flour, salt and baking powder; add the yolks of the eggs and the milk, then the cold cereal, beating this in well to eliminate all lumps.

127

Beat the whites of the eggs to a stiff froth and fold them gently into the batter. Cook at once in hot, lightly-greased waffle irons.

Pound Cake Waffles

¾ cup butter.	1¼ cups flour.
1 cup fine granulated sugar.	1 teaspoon Rumford Baking Powder.
5 eggs.	½ teaspoon salt.

1 teaspoon lemon or vanilla flavoring.

Beat the butter and sugar to a cream; add the well-beaten yolks of the eggs, then the flour, salt and baking powder sifted together. Put in the flavoring and beat the batter thoroughly. At the last moment fold in lightly the whites of the eggs beaten to a stiff froth, and cook as ordinary waffles.

Rye Griddle Cakes

2 cups rye flour.	1 teaspoon salt.
1 cup entire wheat flour.	2 eggs.
3 teaspoons Rumford Baking Powder.	1 pint milk.

Sift together the two flours, salt and baking powder; add the milk and then the eggs well beaten. Beat thoroughly and cook at once on a hot, lightly-greased griddle.

Corn Meal Griddle Cakes

1 cup corn meal.	⅔ teaspoon salt.
Boiling water.	1 tablespoon molasses (if liked).
2 tablespoons flour.	
2 teaspoons Rumford Baking Powder.	1 egg.
	1 cup milk.

Scald the corn meal with just enough boiling water to cover it. Let it stand five minutes, then add flour, salt and molasses. Thin to a batter with the beaten egg and milk, and add the baking powder last, beating it in well. Cook at once on a hot, well-greased griddle.

Rice Griddle Cakes

1 cup warm, boiled rice.	2 tablespoons melted butter.
½ teaspoon salt.	2 eggs
1 cup milk.	2 tablespoons flour.
1 teaspoon Rumford Baking Powder.	

Put the rice in a bowl and add to it the salt, milk, butter and yolks of the eggs; then stir in the flour sifted with the baking powder, and lastly add the stiffly-beaten whites of eggs. Cook quickly on a hot, greased griddle.

Potato Griddle Scones

3 cups flour.	2 tablespoons butter.
½ teaspoon salt.	1 egg.
2 teaspoons Rumford Baking Powder.	About 1 cup milk.
	1 cup mashed potatoes.

Sift together the flour, salt and baking powder; rub the butter in lightly, add the potatoes and mix to a soft dough with the milk and beaten egg. Roll out about three-quarters of an inch thick, cut into three-cornered cakes and cook on a hot, well-greased griddle.

Quick Buckwheat Cakes

1½ cups buckwheat flour.	2 rounding teaspoons Rumford Baking Powder.
1 cup white flour.	
1 egg.	1 teaspoon salt.
1½ cups milk.	

Sift together the buckwheat, flour, salt and baking powder; add the egg well beaten, also the milk gradually. Beat well to remove any lumps, and cook at once on a hot, greased griddle. Two tablespoons of molasses may be added before baking, if desired. This slightly sweetens as well as helps to brown the cakes.

French Pancakes

1 cup flour.	½ teaspoon salt.
1 teaspoon Rumford Bak-	2 eggs.
ing Powder.	1½ cups milk.

Preserve.

Sift together the flour, salt and baking powder; beat and add the eggs with the milk, being careful that there are no lumps. Melt a teaspoon of butter in a frying-pan, and when hot pour in enough batter to just cover the bottom of the pan. Cook golden brown, then turn and cook the other side. Spread with the preserve and roll up and sprinkle with sugar just before serving.

Cream Pancakes

2 tablespoons flour.	⅓ teaspoon salt.
1 teaspoon Rumford Bak-	2 egg yolks.
ing Powder.	1 cup thin cream.

1 tablespoon sugar.

Sift together the flour, salt and baking powder; add the yolks of the eggs, the cream and sugar. Beat well, and cook at once on a hot, lightly-greased griddle. Serve with sugar or maple syrup.

German Pancakes

1 tablespoon butter.	1 heaping tablespoon flour.
4 eggs.	⅓ teaspoon salt.

1 cup milk.

Separate the whites from the yolks of the eggs, beat both thoroughly and add the flour and salt to the yolks. When well mixed stir in the milk and, at the last moment, fold in the stiffly-beaten whites. Melt the butter in a large frying-pan, pour in the batter and cook over a moderately hot fire till it begins to set; then transfer the pan to a hot oven to finish cooking. Turn onto a hot dish and serve with apple sauce.

MEMORANDA

MEMORANDA

CAKE

IN cake making, perhaps even more than in any other branch of cookery, special attention must be paid not only to exact measurements, but to correct methods of manipulation.

Flour, pulverized sugar and similar ingredients must all be sifted once before measuring as they are liable to "pack" in the sack or barrel in which they are kept. Soda, spices and baking powder should be stirred lightly and mixed before measuring, for the same reason.

The ingredients used for cake making should always be the best obtainable: best tub butter, fresh eggs, fine granulated sugar and, preferably, pastry flour, if perfect results are to be obtained. Flours vary in thickening qualities, therefore the exact amount of liquid can not always be stated.

There are three methods of mixing: stirring, beating, and cutting or folding.

In stirring, the spoon is not lifted from the bowl, and the motion may be described as a circular one.

In beating, the object desired is to get all the air possible into the mixture; the faster we beat the more air will be incorporated in the batter, and the cake in consequence will be lighter; but care must be taken that after a cake is beaten, no stirring motion is allowed, as this would undo the good already accomplished.

The term "folding" applies more especially to the mixing and blending of the whites of stiffly-beaten eggs which are added just before putting the cake batter in the pans. The motion is that of lifting the batter from the bottom of the bowl, folding it over the beaten whites, mixing them in and continuing the process till the whites of eggs are no longer seen on top of the batter. The whole process must be performed with great care to avoid destroying the lightness of the air cells in either batter or eggs.

133

In beating butter and sugar to a cream, never warm them nor the bowl, for if the warming is continued a little too long both flavor and texture of the cake will suffer. If the butter is very hard and it is not convenient to leave it in a warm kitchen to soften slowly, a tablespoon of boiling water may be added to the butter and sugar in the bowl, to soften the butter just enough to make it cream readily.

If whites and yolks of eggs are separated, add the whites, well beaten, just before placing the cake in pans. This method makes a lighter, fluffier cake, but one which will dry sooner than if the yolks and whites are beaten together.

Fruit should be washed and thoroughly dried before being added to cake.

Most cake requires a moderately hot oven, but should not be baked too quickly at first. As soon as the cake has risen well the heat may be increased a little to give a good crust. Cake is done as soon as it shrinks a little from the sides of the pan. Another test is to press the centre of the cake with the finger and if firm to the touch, it is ready to come out of the oven. Testing with a broom straw is also a safe rule. If the straw after having been pressed well into the centre of the cake comes out clean, the cake is done. If sticky, bake a little longer.

Lemon Cake

2 scant cups sugar.	2 rounding teaspoons Rumford Baking Powder.
¼ cup butter.	
3 eggs.	Grated rind of 1 lemon.
1 cup milk.	½ teaspoon salt.
3 cups flour.	

Beat the butter with half the sugar; add gradually the remainder of the sugar together with the well-beaten eggs. Next, put in the grated lemon, then the milk, and lastly the flour sifted with the salt and baking powder. Bake about forty minutes in a moderate oven, and cover with lemon frosting.

Chocolate Loaf Cake

1½ cups sugar.
½ cup butter.
2 eggs.
1 cup milk.

2 cups flour.
2 teaspoons Rumford Baking
    Powder.
1 teaspoon vanilla extract.
2 squares chocolate.

Beat to a cream one cup of the sugar with the butter; add the eggs well beaten, then half a cup of the milk and the vanilla. Sift together the flour and baking powder, and beat them into the other ingredients. Put the remainder of the sugar and milk, with the chocolate, into a saucepan and cook till the chocolate is dissolved; add to the cake batter, beat well, and bake in a moderate oven about three-quarters of an hour.

Coffee Chocolate Cake

⅔ cup butter.
2 cups sugar.
2 eggs.
½ cup milk.
1 square chocolate.

½ cup strong coffee.
3 cups flour.
2 teaspoons Rumford Baking
    Powder.
½ teaspoon salt.
1 teaspoon vanilla extract.

Beat the butter and sugar till light and creamy, adding the well-beaten yolks of the eggs as soon as the butter and sugar are well mixed; then put in the chocolate, which has been softened by standing over hot water, the coffee and milk. Add the flour, baking powder and salt sifted together, and then the vanilla. Beat vigorously and at the last moment before baking fold in the stiffly-beaten whites of the eggs. Bake about three-quarters of an hour in two loaf-cake pans, having the oven moderately hot. Frost, if desired.

White Cake

1 cup butter.
2 cups pulverized sugar.
1 cup milk.
2 cups flour.

½ teaspoon salt.
2 teaspoons Rumford Baking
    Powder.
7 egg whites.

Beat the butter and sugar to a cream; add the milk, then the flour, salt and baking powder sifted together;

fold in very gently the stiffly-beaten whites of the eggs and turn into a greased pan. Bake in a moderate oven about three-quarters of an hour.

Sultana Cake

2 cups flour.	½ cup sugar.
2 teaspoons Rumford Baking Powder.	½ cup sultana raisins.
⅓ teaspoon salt.	1 egg.
⅓ cup butter.	⅓ cup chopped citron or lemon peel.

About ¾ cup milk.

Sift together the flour, salt and baking powder; rub in the butter and then add the sugar, raisins and citron. Beat the egg well, and add it with the milk. Turn into a well-greased pan, and bake about forty-five minutes.

Honey Cake

⅓ cup butter.	2 cups flour.
½ cup sugar.	1½ teaspoons Rumford Baking Powder.
2 eggs.	
1 cup honey.	⅓ teaspoon salt.

Beat the butter and sugar till creamy; add the eggs well beaten, then the honey, and lastly the flour sifted with the baking powder and salt. Bake in a loaf-cake pan in a moderate oven about forty minutes.

Gold Loaf Cake

½ cup butter.	½ cup milk.
1 cup fine granulated sugar.	1¾ cups flour.
7 egg yolks.	2 teaspoons Rumford Baking Powder.

½ teaspoon vanilla flavoring.

Beat the butter and sugar till creamy; add the yolks of eggs beaten till thick and then put in the milk. Sift together the flour and baking powder twice and add to the other ingredients with the flavoring; beat well and pour into a pan with loose bottom or removable sides. Bake in a moderate oven about three-quarters of an hour.

Nut Cake

⅔ cup butter.
1 cup sugar.
6 egg yolks.
¼ cup milk.
1 cup chopped nuts.

2½ cups flour.
2 teaspoons Rumford Baking
    Powder.
⅓ teaspoon salt.
1 teaspoon almond extract.

Beat the butter and sugar to a cream; add the well-beaten yolks of the eggs, then the milk, chopped nuts and extract. Sift together the flour, baking powder and salt and add to the other ingredients. Bake in a loaf-cake pan in a moderate oven about forty minutes.

Cornstarch Cake

½ cup butter.
1 cup sugar.
½ cup milk.
½ cup cornstarch.

1½ cups flour.
⅓ teaspoon salt.
2 teaspoons Rumford Baking
    Powder.

6 egg whites.

Cream the butter and sugar well together; add the milk, then the cornstarch and flour sifted with the salt and baking powder. Add lastly the whites of the eggs beaten to a stiff froth. Bake about forty-five minutes in a moderate oven, using rather shallow pans.

Devil Cake

½ cup butter.
2 cups sugar.
3 cups sifted flour.
3 level teaspoons Rumford
    Baking Powder.
½ teaspoon ground cloves.
½ teaspoon ground nutmeg.

1 cup cold water.
1 square unsweetened choco-
    late.
4 egg whites.
1 teaspoon each vanilla and
    lemon extracts.

Cream the butter, add the sugar and beat together for five minutes. Sift together flour, baking powder and spices and add them to the butter and sugar with the water. Melt the chocolate in a cup over boiling water and beat into the cake with the flavoring. Then fold in the whites of the eggs beaten to a stiff froth. Bake in a greased pan in a moderate oven from thirty to forty-five minutes. Cover with boiled frosting.

Poor Man's Cake

1 cup sugar.	2 teaspoons Rumford Baking
1 egg.	Powder.
2 tablespoons butter.	1 teaspoon vanilla or other
1 cup milk.	extract.
	2 cups flour.

Beat the egg and sugar together till light; add the milk, then the melted butter and extract. Sift the flour and baking powder twice, add the liquid mixture to them and beat well. Bake about forty-five minutes in a moderate oven.

Pound Cake

2 cups butter.	4 scant cups pastry flour.
2 cups granulated sugar.	¼ grated nutmeg.
10 eggs.	½ teaspoon salt.

Beat the butter and sugar till very light and creamy; add the well-beaten yolks of eggs. Sift together twice the flour, salt and nutmeg and add a little at a time. Whip the whites of eggs till very stiff and fold them into the cake batter as gently as possible.

Line cake pans with paper, fill two-thirds full with the batter, and bake in a moderate oven about one and one-half hours.

Plain Cocoanut Cake

⅓ cup butter.	1 cup cocoanut fresh or
1 cup sugar.	dried.
2 eggs.	⅓ teaspoon salt.
½ cup milk.	2 cups flour.
	2 teaspoons Rumford Baking Powder.

Beat the butter with half the sugar; add the well-beaten eggs and remaining sugar, then the milk and cocoanut and, lastly, the flour, salt and baking powder sifted together. Beat well, and bake either

as a loaf or layer cake. If fresh-grated cocoanut is
used a little less milk will probably be required.

Inexpensive Fruit Cake

2 cups flour.	1 teaspoon ground cinnamon.
2 teaspoons Rumford Baking Powder.	¼ cup butter.
	1 cup sugar.
¼ teaspoon ground cloves.	1 cup milk.
½ teaspoon ground nutmeg.	1 egg.
	½ cup raisins.
½ teaspoon salt.	½ cup currants.

Sift together the flour, salt, spices and baking
powder; rub in the butter and add the sugar and
fruit. Mix to soft dough with the egg and milk,
and bake in a loaf-cake pan in a moderate oven
about three-quarters of an hour.

White Fruit Cake

1 cup butter.	1 cup milk.
2 cups sugar.	6 egg whites.
1 cup grated cocoanut.	3 cups flour.
1½ cups blanched and chopped almonds.	½ teaspoon salt.
	2 teaspoons Rumford Baking Powder.
½ cup mixed candied peel, cut small.	

Beat the butter and sugar to a cream; add the
cocoanut, almonds and peel, and then the milk. Beat
the whites of the eggs to a stiff froth and add with
the flour, salt and baking powder sifted together,
folding them in as gently as possible. Bake in loaf-
cake pans in a steady oven about forty-five minutes.

Rich Fruit Cake

¾ pound butter.	½ cup molasses.
1 pound brown sugar.	½ ounce cloves.
8 eggs.	½ ounce cinnamon.
2 pounds raisins.	¼ ounce mace.
2 pounds currants.	4 cups flour.
1 pound citron chopped very fine.	1 wineglass sherry.
	1 wineglass brandy.

Beat the butter and sugar till light and creamy;
add the eggs thoroughly beaten, then the raisins

(seeded) and currants well washed and dried. Chop the citron — or pass it through a meat chopper — and add to the other ingredients with the molasses and ground spices. Sift and add the flour and, lastly, stir in the sherry and brandy. Bake in cake pans lined with two thicknesses of greased paper to protect the cake from too great heat. Bake very slowly about four hours.

Wedding Fruit Cake

1 pound citron.	6 eggs.
1 pound candied apricots.	1 pound flour.
1 pound candied pineapple.	1 teaspoon Rumford Baking
1 pound candied cherries.	Powder.
3 pounds seeded raisins.	2 teaspoons cinnamon.
1½ pounds currants.	½ teaspoon cloves.
½ pound butter.	1 nutmeg.
½ pound brown sugar.	⅓ teaspoon salt.
½ cup brandy.	

Cut the citron, apricots and pineapple in large pieces, leaving the cherries whole. Seed the raisins, and wash and dry the currants. Cream the butter and sugar, add the yolks of eggs well beaten, then the fruit, also the flour, salt, baking powder and spices sifted together; put in the brandy and mix all thoroughly. Last of all add the stiffly-beaten whites of the eggs. Turn into greased cake pans and steam five hours; afterwards bake very slowly for one hour to slightly dry the cake.

Yorkshire Parkin

1½ cups flour.	¾ cup sugar.
2 cups oatmeal.	2 teaspoons Rumford Baking
1 cup molasses.	Powder.
1 egg.	1 teaspoon soda.
⅓ cup butter.	1 teaspoon ground ginger.
½ cup milk.	

Sift together the flour, baking powder and ginger, and then add the sugar and oatmeal. Heat the butter and molasses to the boiling point, add to the dry ingredients with the egg and milk, add also the soda dissolved in a tablespoon of hot water. Beat well, turn into a well-greased, shallow pan and bake slowly about one and one-half hours.

Scotch Shortbread

3 cups flour.	1 cup sugar.
2 cups butter.	1 ounce blanched almonds.

Sift the flour twice and rub in the butter with the hands; add the sugar and knead and mix, either on a board or in a bowl, till a dough is formed. Do not add either egg or milk, as the butter softens from the mixing and will bind the ingredients together. Roll the dough rather thinly, cut into rounds or ovals and press a few almonds into each. Place on a flat baking-pan, and bake in a slow oven till golden brown.

Quick German Coffee Cake

2¼ cups sifted flour.	1 egg.
1 teaspoon salt.	1½ cups milk.
2 heaping teaspoons Rumford Baking Powder.	Melted butter.
2 tablespoons sugar.	Cinnamon and sugar to sprinkle over the top.

Sift together the flour, salt and baking powder; add the sugar and mix all to a soft dough with the beaten egg and milk. Beat well and turn into a greased biscuit pan; spread evenly, brush over with melted butter and sprinkle with cinnamon and sugar. Bake in a moderate oven about twenty-five minutes.

German Apple Cake

2 cups flour.	3 tablespoons butter.
½ teaspoon salt.	1 egg.
2 level teaspoons Rumford Baking Powder.	About 1 cup milk.
	Apples.
Sugar.	

Sift together the flour, salt and baking powder; rub in the butter and mix to a light dough with the beaten egg and milk. Roll out about half an inch thick and lay on a greased, shallow baking-pan. Pare and core the apples, cut into eighths, lay the pieces on the dough and sprinkle with sugar to taste. Bake about half an hour in a moderate oven, and serve hot with whipped cream.

Plain Sponge Cake

3 eggs.	1 teaspoon Rumford Baking
1 cup sugar.	Powder.
½ cup hot water.	⅓ teaspoon salt.
1 cup sifted flour.	Grated rind of half a lemon.

Beat the eggs, with half the sugar, till they thicken; add the water and remainder of the sugar, and beat again. Put in the grated lemon rind, then the flour sifted with the salt and baking powder, folding these in as gently as possible. Bake about thirty minutes in a shallow pan that has been greased and floured.

Old-fashioned Sponge Cake

10 eggs.	1½ cups flour.
2 cups fine granulated sugar.	1 teaspoon of any desired flavoring.

Separate the whites from the yolks of the eggs and beat the yolks with the sugar till they are thick and ropy. Next, beat the whites till stiff and add them with the flavoring. As soon as mixed fold in the flour very gently, mixing just enough to blend it with the other ingredients. Butter a deep cake pan and sprinkle with flour, shaking off all that does not cling to the pan. Pour the cake batter into the pan, filling it not more than two-thirds, and bake in a moderately quick oven about three-quarters of an hour.

Pineapple Cake

5 eggs.	¼ pound glacé pineapple.
1 cup pulverized sugar.	1 cup pastry flour.

Put the eggs and sugar into a large bowl and beat till very thick. Sift the flour twice and add it to the eggs and sugar. Cut the fruit into shreds, toss in flour to keep them separate, and add to the cake; mix lightly and pour into a shallow pan lined with greased paper. Bake from twenty minutes to half an hour in a moderately hot oven. Frost when cold, if desired.

Jelly Roll

3 eggs.	1 cup flour.
1 cup sugar.	1 teaspoon Rumford Baking
3 tablespoons cold water.	Powder.
	⅓ teaspoon salt.

Beat the eggs and sugar till quite thick; add the water, then the flour, salt and baking powder sifted together twice. Line a shallow pan with greased paper, pour in the batter evenly, and bake in a quick oven about twelve minutes. Turn out onto a cloth or paper sprinkled with sugar, tear off the paper and spread with jam or jelly. Roll up quickly.

Eggless Cake

½ cup butter.	2 teaspoons Rumford Baking
1½ cups sugar.	Powder.
1 cup milk.	1 cup currants or raisins.
3 cups flour.	½ teaspoon mixed spices.
	⅓ teaspoon salt.

Beat the butter and sugar till light and creamy; add the milk, then the fruit and, lastly, the flour, salt, baking powder and spices sifted together. Turn into a greased pan and bake in a slow oven about one hour.

Orange-Cocoanut Cake

2 cups sugar.	Juice and grated rind of
1 cup butter.	1 orange.
3 egg whites.	2 cups flour.
5 yolks.	½ cup water.
	1¼ teaspoons Rumford Baking Powder.

Beat the butter and sugar to a cream; add the yolks of eggs and water, then the juice and rind of the orange; next, the flour and baking powder sifted together, and fold in very gently the stiffly-beaten whites of the eggs. Bake twenty minutes in a hot oven in layer-cake pans, and put the layers together with Orange and Cocoanut Filling.

Plain Loaf Cake

½ cup butter.
1 cup sugar.
2 eggs.
½ cup milk.

1 teaspoon lemon or
  vanilla extract
2 cups flour.
2 level teaspoons Rumford
  Baking Powder.

Beat the butter and sugar till light and creamy; add the well-beaten eggs, then the milk and flavoring extract, and, lastly, the flour and baking powder sifted together. Beat well, and bake in a loaf-cake pan about forty-five minutes.

Lily Cake

⅓ cup butter.
1 cup sugar.
½ cup milk.
1¾ cups flour.
3 egg whites.

2½ teaspoons Rumford Baking Powder.
⅓ teaspoon lemon extract.
⅔ teaspoon vanilla extract.

Cream the butter gradually and add the sugar; next, the milk and flavorings, then the flour sifted with the baking powder and beat well. Add the whites of the eggs whipped to a stiff froth and bake in layers twenty minutes. Fill with Prune Almond Filling.

Lady Baltimore Cake

1½ cups fine granulated
  sugar.
1 scant cup butter.
1 cup milk.

3 cups flour.
2 teaspoons Rumford Baking
  Powder.
6 egg whites.

Beat the butter and sugar till very light and creamy; add the milk alternately with the flour with which the baking powder has been sifted. Beat thoroughly, and add the stiffly-beaten whites of the eggs. Bake about forty minutes in two lightly-greased pans, and fill with Lady Baltimore Filling.

Fig Layer Cake

¼ cup butter.
1 cup sugar.
1 egg.
1 cup milk.

½ cup finely-chopped figs.
2 cups flour.
⅓ teaspoon salt.
2 teaspoons Rumford Baking
   Powder.

Beat the butter and sugar till creamy; add the beaten egg and milk, then the figs and, lastly, the flour, salt and baking powder sifted together. Bake in layers about twenty minutes, and fill with Fig Filling.

Coffee Layer Cake

¼ cup butter.
1 cup brown sugar
2 eggs.
½ cup molasses.
½ cup made coffee.

2 cups flour.
½ teaspoon mixed spices.
½ teaspoon salt.
2 teaspoons Rumford Baking
   Powder.

Beat the butter and sugar till creamy; add the eggs, then the molasses and coffee and, lastly, the flour, salt, spices and baking powder sifted together. Bake in layers about twenty minutes, and put together with frosting.

Marshmallow Cake

1 cup sugar.
½ cup butter.
2 eggs.
1 cup milk.

2½ cups flour.
2 teaspoons Rumford Baking
   Powder.
½ teaspoon salt.

1 teaspoon vanilla extract.

Beat the butter and sugar to a cream; add the yolks of the eggs well beaten, the milk, and then the flour, salt and baking powder sifted together twice. Next, put in the vanilla and beat the cake well; then fold in gently the whites of the eggs whipped to a stiff froth. Bake in two layer-cake pans about twenty minutes, and put together with Marshmallow Filling.

White Layer Cake

½ cup butter.
1½ cups sugar.
½ cup milk.
1½ cups flour.

1 teaspoon Rumford Baking
  Powder.
⅓ teaspoon salt.
1 teaspoon flavoring extract.
4 egg whites.

Beat the butter and sugar to a cream; add the milk and flavoring, then the flour, salt and baking powder sifted together. Beat very thoroughly, and then fold in very gently the stiffly-beaten whites of the eggs. Bake about twenty minutes in layer-cake pans, putting the layers together with any desired filling.

Layer Cake No. 1

½ cup butter.
2 cups sugar.
4 eggs.
1 cup cold water.

3 cups flour.
2 teaspoons Rumford Baking
  Powder.
⅓ teaspoon salt.
1 teaspoon vanilla.

Beat the butter and sugar till creamy; add the yolks of the eggs well beaten, then the water and flavoring and, next, the flour, salt and baking powder sifted together. Beat the whites of the eggs to a stiff froth and add them last. Bake about twenty minutes in layer-cake pans, and put together with any desired filling.

Layer Cake No. 2

2 eggs.
1 cup sugar.
½ cup water or milk.
2 cups flour.

¼ teaspoon salt.
2 teaspoons Rumford Baking
  Powder.
1 teaspoon flavoring extract.

Beat the eggs and sugar till light and frothy; add the water or milk, then the flour, salt and baking powder which have been sifted together twice. Add the flavoring and bake about twenty minutes in greased layer-cake pans, and put together with any desired filling.

This cake dries more quickly than one in which butter is used.

Date Lunch Cake

½ cup butter.
1 cup sugar.
2 eggs.
1 cup milk.
3 cups flour.
¼ teaspoon salt.
2 teaspoons Rumford Baking
    Powder.
1½ cups dates, stoned and cut in pieces.

Beat the butter and sugar till light; add the eggs well beaten, then the dates, milk and, lastly, the flour, salt and baking powder sifted together. Beat well, and bake in a shallow, greased pan in a quick oven. Cut in squares before serving.

English Walnut Cake

¼ cup butter.
1 cup sifted powdered
    sugar.
6 egg yolks.
2 level tablespoons sifted
    cocoa.
1 level teaspoon cinnamon.
¼ teaspoon cloves.
⅛ teaspoon nutmeg.
1 cup English walnuts,
    finely chopped.
1 cup soft bread crumbs.
2 teaspoons Rumford Baking Powder.

Cream the butter, add the sugar, and the yolks of the eggs well beaten, then the cocoa and ground spices sifted together; put in next the walnuts, and beat all thoroughly. Stir in the bread crumbs with which the baking powder has been mixed, and fold in lightly the whites of the eggs beaten till stiff and dry. Bake at once in layer-cake pans, and put the layers together with Orange Walnut Filling.

Layers for Mocha Cake

¼ cup butter.
2 cups sugar.
¾ cup milk.
1 teaspoon vanilla extract.
6 egg whites.
2½ cups flour.
¼ teaspoon salt.
2 teaspoons Rumford Baking
    Powder.

Beat the butter and sugar to a cream; add the milk and vanilla, then the flour, salt and baking powder sifted together and, lastly, fold in very gently the

whites of the eggs beaten to a stiff froth.   Bake in
layer-cake pans, and fill with Mocha Filling.

Queen Cakes

1 cup butter.	3 cups flour.
2 cups sugar.	½ teaspoon salt.
4 eggs.	2 teaspoons Rumford Baking
1 cup seeded raisins.	Powder.
1 cup milk.	

Beat the butter and sugar to a cream; add the
yolks of the eggs well beaten, the fruit and milk, and
then the flour with which the salt and baking powder
have been sifted.   Lastly, fold in gently the whites
of the eggs beaten to a stiff froth.   Bake in a hot
oven in well-greased fancy pans about twelve minutes.

Lady Fingers

2 egg yolks.	⅓ cup pastry flour.
3 egg whites.	⅓ teaspoon salt.
⅓ cup powdered sugar.	¼ teaspoon vanilla extract.

Beat the whites of the eggs till very stiff, adding
the sugar gradually.   Then add the well-beaten yolks
and the vanilla; fold in very gently the flour sifted
with the salt.   Force the mixture through a pastry
bag onto a greased, flat pan; sprinkle well with sifted
sugar, and bake eight minutes in a moderate oven.

New Year's Cakes

1 quart flour.	1 cup butter.
1 teaspoon salt.	2 cups sugar.
3 teaspoons Rumford Bak-	1 tablespoon caraway seeds.
ing Powder.	1 egg.
	1½ cups milk.

Sift together the flour, salt and baking powder; rub
in the butter with the fingers, then add the sugar and
seeds and mix to a light dough with the egg, and the
milk slightly warmed.   Knead till smooth, roll thinly
and cut into any desired shape.   Bake on flat tins in
a hot oven about fifteen minutes.

Queen Eclairs

¼ cup water.
1 tablespoon butter.
¼ cup flour.
⅓ teaspoon salt.

3 eggs.
1 teaspoon Rumford Baking
  Powder.

Put the water and butter into a saucepan and allow them to boil; stir in the flour and salt and cook till the mixture forms a stiff paste and leaves the sides of the saucepan clean. Cool slightly, and beat in the eggs one at a time. Add the baking powder last, and force the mixture through a pastry bag onto flat, greased pans, in pieces about the width of two fingers and length of one. Bake slowly till quite light. Cool, make an incision in the side of each eclair and fill with whipped cream or custard. They may be iced, if desired, with Chocolate or Coffee Frosting.

Fairy Cones

6 egg yolks.
3 tablespoons sugar.
2 tablespoons flour.

1 cup chopped English walnut meats.
Whipped cream, sweetened
  and flavored.

Beat the yolks of the eggs with the sugar; add the flour, then the nuts and spread as thinly as possible on greased, flat baking-tins. Bake about seven minutes, and while still warm cut into squares and roll each in the form of a cone. When wanted for use fill with the sweetened and flavored whipped cream.

Cream Puffs

1 cup boiling water.
½ teaspoon salt.
⅓ cup butter.

1½ cups flour.
4 eggs.
Whipped cream or custard.

Bring the water, salt and butter together to boiling point; stir in the flour and cook till the mixture leaves the sides of the saucepan clean. When cooled, add the eggs one at a time, beating each one in thoroughly; drop by tablespoonfuls some distance apart on greased baking-pans, and bake half an hour in a steady oven. When cold, split and fill with sweetened cream or thick custard.

Pecan Sticks

⅔ cup butter.
⅔ cup sugar.
2 eggs.
½ cup milk.
1 cup shelled pecan nuts.

1½ cups flour.
½ teaspoon salt.
1½ teaspoons Rumford Baking Powder.

Beat the butter and sugar to a cream; add the eggs well beaten, the milk and nuts, and then the flour, salt and baking powder sifted together. Beat thoroughly, and bake in greased finger-roll pans. When cold, cover the tops with a white frosting into which a few extra nuts have been stirred.

Moon Cakes

½ cup butter.
⅔ cup sugar.
2 eggs.
⅓ cup blanched and chopped almonds.

⅓ teaspoon salt.
1½ cups flour.
1 teaspoon Rumford Baking Powder.

Beat the butter and sugar to a cream; add the well-beaten eggs, then the almonds and, lastly, the flour, salt and baking powder sifted together. Bake in a hot oven in lightly-greased, crescent-shaped pans. Frost, if desired.

Rollemups

2 cups flour.
⅓ teaspoon salt.
2 teaspoons Rumford Baking Powder.
2 tablespoons butter.
1 egg.

1 cup milk.
¼ cup maple sugar, or
¾ cup brown sugar and
½ teaspoon ground cinnamon.

Sift together the flour, salt and baking powder; rub in the butter, add the sugar and mix to a soft dough with the egg and milk. Roll half an inch thick on a floured board, sprinkle with the maple sugar — or brown sugar and cinnamon — and roll into a long roll. Press the edges closely together and cut into three-fourths inch slices with a sharp knife and lay cut side down on a greased pan. Bake about twenty minutes in a quick oven.

MEMORANDA

MEMORANDA

CAKE FILLINGS, FROSTINGS AND ICINGS

Fig Filling

1 pound figs.	2 tablespoons sugar.
1 cup water.	Juice of 1 lemon.

Pass the figs through the medium cutter of a meat chopper, add the water and sugar, and cook till they form a thick pulp. Add the lemon juice, beat well and, when cool, spread between the layers of cake.

Almond Filling

3 egg yolks.	⅔ cup almonds, or
2 cups confectioners' sugar.	½ cup almond paste.
1 teaspoon coffee extract.	

Beat the yolks of the eggs till thick, add the sugar thoroughly sifted, then the almonds passed through the finest knives of a meat chopper, or, better still, use almond paste. Flavor with the coffee extract, and spread between layers of cake.

Maple Filling

1 cup thin cream.	2 cups scraped maple sugar.
½ cup chopped nuts.	

Cook the cream and maple sugar slowly till they thicken; remove from the fire, add the nuts, and beat till creamy before filling the cake.

Orange and Walnut Filling

½ pound English walnuts.	Juice and pulp of 1 orange.
1 cup powdered sugar.	

Shell the nuts, reserving a few unbroken halves for the top of the cake. Put the orange pulp and juice

153

into a bowl, add the sugar, cook three minutes, cool, and then beat till it thickens; add the chopped nuts and spread between layers of cake. Frost the top with Plain Orange Icing, and decorate with the halves of nuts.

Orange and Cocoanut Filling

1 egg.	1 cup grated cocoanut.
1 cup whipped cream.	Grated rind of 1 orange.
½ cup powdered sugar.	Juice of 1 orange.

Beat the egg until light, add the whipped cream and sugar, then the orange rind, cocoanut and orange juice. Spread between and on top of layers of cake.

Portsmouth Orange Filling

1 cube cut sugar.	2 tablespoons water.
1 orange.	About 2 cups confectioners'
Juice of 1 lemon.	sugar.

Rub the sugar over the rind of the orange, then dissolve the sugar with the juice of the lemon and water, and strain; add the confectioners' sugar, using enough to make a thick icing. Spread the icing between the layers of cake and imbed in it very thin slices of orange, skinned and seeded. Cover with more of the icing, and decorate with sections of tangerine or glacé oranges.

Lady Baltimore Filling

2 cups granulated sugar.	2 egg whites.
1 cup water.	1 cup chopped raisins.
	1 cup chopped nuts.

Boil the sugar and water five minutes, pour the boiling syrup over the whites of the eggs which have been beaten till stiff, and set aside half of the mixture for the frosting. Add the raisins and nuts to the remainder and use for the filling.

Mocha Filling and Frosting

6 tablespoons butter.   4 tablespoons dry cocoa.
2 cups confectioners'   3 tablespoons liquid coffee.
   sugar.   1 teaspoon vanilla extract.

Beat the butter to a cream, adding one cup of the sugar; then sift and add the cocoa. Beat well, put in the coffee and remaining sugar, and then the vanilla. Spread between and on top of layers of cake.

Caramel Nut Filling

1 cup thin cream.   1 cup brown sugar.
1 cup nuts, coarsely chopped.

Cook the cream and sugar slowly till they begin to thicken. Remove from the fire, stir until creamy, add the nuts and spread between layers of cake.

Marshmallow Filling

¾ cup sugar.   ¼ pound marshmallows.
¼ cup milk.   2 tablespoons boiling water.
1 teaspoon vanilla.

Put the sugar and milk into a saucepan, bring to the boiling point and boil six minutes without stirring. Melt the marshmallows in a double boiler, add the boiling water and cook till smooth; then add the hot syrup, beating while adding. Add the vanilla and beat till cool enough to spread. Use for both filling and frosting.

Prune Almond Filling

1 cup sugar.   1 egg white.
⅓ cup boiling water.   ½ cup prunes.
⅓ cup blanched almonds.

Boil the sugar and water together, without stirring, till a little lifted on a spoon forms a thread, and pour this over the beaten white of the egg, beating while adding. Add the prunes which have been cooked till soft, stoned and cut in pieces; also the almonds, blanched and chopped. When cold spread between layers of cake.

Chocolate Frosting

2 squares chocolate.	3 tablespoons boiling
6 tablespoons confec-	water.
tioners' sugar.	

Melt the chocolate in a double boiler, add the sugar and water and cook gently till smooth. Cool, and spread on cake.

Lemon Frosting

Juice of 2 lemons.	About 2½ cups powdered
	sugar.

Strain the juice of the lemons into a bowl and add the sugar, finely sifted, until thick enough to spread. The exact quantity of sugar will depend on the size of the lemons. Pour over the top of the cake, and spread and smooth with a thin-bladed knife that has been dipped in water.

Boiled Frosting

1 cup granulated sugar.	1 egg white.
⅓ cup hot water.	⅛ teaspoon cream of tartar.
	1 teaspoon flavoring.

Boil the sugar and water together, without stirring, till they form a thread when a little is lifted from the pan; beat the white of the egg, add the cream of tartar and pour the hot syrup over them, beating while doing so. Add the flavoring, and beat till thick enough to spread.

Plain Orange Icing

Grated rind and strained	About 1½ cups powdered
juice of 1 orange.	sugar.

Put the rind and juice of the orange into a bowl, add the sugar (sifted) till the mixture is thick enough to spread. Beat well and pour over the cake. Smooth with a thin-bladed knife that has been dipped in water.

Coffee Icing

½ cup strong, clear coffee.   2 cups granulated sugar.
2 teaspoons vanilla extract.

Cook the coffee and sugar together till a little dropped in cold water forms a soft ball. Cool, add the vanilla, and beat till stiff enough to spread.

Opera Caramel Icing

1½ cups brown sugar.   1 tablespoon butter.
¼ cup thin cream or milk.   Flavoring.

Put the sugar, cream (or milk) and butter into a saucepan and cook gently till a little dropped in cold water forms a soft ball. Remove from the fire, cool, add the flavoring, and beat till thick enough to spread.

Fondant Icing

2 cups granulated sugar.   1 cup boiling water.
Flavoring.

Put the sugar and water together in a saucepan and stir till the sugar is dissolved. Then put over the fire and cook, without stirring or shaking, till a little dropped in cold water forms a soft ball. Remove at once from the fire and cool, still without stirring as this would cause the sugar to grain. When cool add the flavoring, beat till creamy, then knead with the hands till very smooth. This creamy fondant is better if allowed to stand a few days before using, and will keep indefinitely if covered with a damp cloth or waxed paper. When required for use put the desired quantity in a bowl over hot water, and melt till soft enough to spread.

Milk Frosting

1½ cups sugar.	½ cup milk.
1 teaspoon butter.	½ teaspoon vanilla.

Melt the butter in a saucepan, then add sugar and milk. Boil gently, without stirring, for thirteen minutes. Beat until stiff enough to spread; then add flavoring, and spread over cake.

MEMORANDA

MEMORANDA

GINGERBREAD, COOKIES, DOUGH-NUTS, ETC.

Dark Gingerbread

½ cup butter.
1 cup molasses.
1 egg.
2 tablespoons milk.

2 cups flour.
½ teaspoon salt.
2 teaspoons ground ginger.
2 teaspoons Rumford Baking Powder.

Heat the butter till hissing, pour it into a bowl in which the molasses has already been measured, add the egg and milk, and mix lightly. Sift together the flour, salt, ginger and baking powder, and stir in the liquid ingredients, beating and stirring only enough to blend. As soon as smoothly blended pour into two shallow, well-greased pans, and bake twenty minutes in a moderately hot oven.

Soft Gingerbread

1 cup New Orleans molasses.
1 cup sugar.
½ cup butter, melted.
1 teaspoon ground ginger.
1 teaspoon soda.

½ teaspoon ground cinnamon.
1 cup water.
4 cups flour.
½ teaspoon salt.

Stir the molasses, sugar and butter together; add the water, then the flour, salt, soda and spices sifted together, and beat hard. Bake in two well-greased pans in a moderate oven about half an hour.

Fruit Gingerbread

½ cup butter.
1 cup sugar.
2 eggs.
1 cup molasses.
3 cups flour.
1¼ teaspoons ginger.

2 teaspoons Rumford Baking Powder.
1 cup seeded raisins.
⅓ cup chopped lemon or orange peel.
½ cup milk or cold coffee.

Beat the butter and sugar till light and creamy; add the beaten yolks of the eggs, then the raisins, peel,

161

molasses and coffee, also the flour with which the ginger and baking powder have been sifted. Then add the whites of the eggs beaten to a stiff froth. Bake in well-greased pans in a moderate oven.

Dropped Cookies

½ cup butter.
1 cup sugar.
2 eggs.
½ cup milk.
¼ cup molasses.

¾ cup currants.
3 cups flour.
2 teaspoons Rumford Baking Powder.
1 teaspoon ground cinnamon.
½ teaspoon ground cloves.

Beat the butter and sugar to a cream; add the well-beaten eggs, then the milk, molasses and currants and, lastly, the dry ingredients well sifted together. Drop by spoonfuls on greased pans, some distance apart. Bake about ten minutes in a moderate oven.

Seed Cookies

1 cup butter.
2 cups sugar.
2 eggs.
½ cup water.

3 cups flour.
½ teaspoon salt.
2 teaspoons Rumford Baking Powder.
2 tablespoons caraway seeds.

Cream the butter and sugar together; add the well-beaten eggs and water. Sift together and add the flour, salt and baking powder, and then the seeds. Turn onto a well-floured board, roll out thinly, cut into rounds and lay on greased, flat pans. Bake about ten minutes in a moderate oven.

Chocolate Cookies

½ cup butter.
1 cup sugar.
1 egg.
2 squares chocolate, melted

¼ cup milk.
2 cups flour.
⅓ teaspoon salt.
1½ teaspoons Rumford Baking Powder.

Beat the butter and sugar to a cream; add the egg, then the melted chocolate and milk. Sift together the flour, salt and baking powder and add to the other ingredients. Roll out thinly, cut into rounds and bake on greased pans in a hot oven.

Sugar Cakes

½ cup butter. 1 cup sugar.
1 cup flour. 2 egg whites.

Rub the butter into the flour and add the sugar, reserving a little to sprinkle over the tops of the cakes. Beat the whites of the eggs lightly and use them to mix the dry ingredients to a dough; roll out thinly and cut into small cakes. Sprinkle with the sugar reserved for the purpose, and bake on greased tins, in a moderate oven, till golden brown.

Jumbles

⅓ cup butter. 1 cup flour.
½ cup sugar. ⅓ teaspoon salt.
1 egg. 1 teaspoon Rumford Baking
Grated rind of half a lemon. Powder.

Beat the butter and sugar to a cream; add the egg previously beaten, the lemon rind, and then the flour, salt and baking powder sifted together. Drop by spoonfuls on a greased pan and bake about ten minutes.

Crullers

½ cup butter. About 3 cups flour.
1 cup sugar. ⅓ teaspoon salt.
2 eggs. 3 teaspoons Rumford Baking
1 cup milk. Powder.
⅓ teaspoon grated nutmeg.

Beat the butter and sugar together; add the beaten eggs and milk, then the flour, salt, baking powder and

nutmeg sifted together.   Roll out, cut, and fry golden
brown in deep fat.   Drain, and sprinkle with sugar.

German Crullers

2 eggs.	½ teaspoon cinnamon or
1 cup milk.	nutmeg.
1 tablespoon melted butter.	⅓ teaspoon salt.
3 cups flour.	1 cup sugar.
2 teaspoons Rumford Baking Powder.	

Beat the eggs till light and mix them with the milk
and butter.   Sift together the flour, salt, spice and
baking powder; add the sugar and blend the two
mixtures.   Roll out, cut into rings and fry in hot fat
till golden brown.   Drain well and dust with sugar.

Sponge Drops

3 eggs.	⅓ teaspoon salt.
¾ cup sugar.	1 teaspoon Rumford Baking
1 cup flour.	Powder.

Beat the eggs till very light; add the sugar and beat
again; fold in gently the flour, salt and baking powder
sifted together.   Drop by teaspoonfuls on greased
pans, some distance apart.   Bake in a hot oven till
set.

Cinnamon Crisps

⅓ cup butter.	1½ cups flour.
⅔ cup sugar.	1 teaspoon Rumford Baking
1 teaspoon cinnamon.	Powder.
¼ cup milk.	

Beat the butter and sugar, and when light and
creamy add the cinnamon, flour and baking powder
sifted together.   Use just enough milk to make a
dough that can be easily rolled out.   Roll very thin

on a well-floured board and cut into squares or rounds. Bake on greased pans, in a moderate oven, about ten minutes.

Oatmeal Crisps

¼ cup butter.
¾ cup flour.
⅓ teaspoon salt.
1 teaspoon Rumford Bak-
   ing Powder.

⅓ cup sugar.
½ cup oatmeal or rolled
   oats.
1 small egg.
A little milk, if needed.

Sift together the flour, salt and baking powder; rub in the butter, add the sugar and oatmeal and mix to a rather stiff dough with the egg, adding milk if necessary. Roll out on a floured board, cut into rounds, and bake about twelve minutes in a moderately hot oven.

Whole Wheat Crisps

¼ cup sugar.
2 cups whole wheat flour.
½ teaspoon salt.

1 teaspoon Rumford Baking
   Powder.
1 cup thin cream.

Sift the flour, salt and baking powder; add the sugar and mix to a stiff dough with the cream; roll very thin and cut out with a biscuit cutter. Bake on greased tins in a hot oven.

Brandy Wafers

1 cup molasses.
¼ cup butter.
    1 teaspoon ground ginger.

1 cup flour.
¾ cup sugar.

Melt the molasses and butter; add the sugar, then the flour and ginger sifted together. Mix well and drop by spoonfuls on well-greased tins, some distance apart. Bake in a moderate oven about ten minutes. Remove from the pans before they become too cool.

Mignons

½ cup butter.
½ cup sugar.
3 egg yolks.
¼ cup blanched almonds,
    pounded fine.
1½ cups sifted flour.

1 teaspoon Rumford Baking
    Powder.
½ teaspoon ground cinna-
    mon.
½ teaspoon vanilla extract.
A little milk, if necessary.

Cream the butter and sugar; add the well-beaten yolks of the eggs, then the almonds and vanilla. Sift together the flour, baking powder and cinnamon, and add to the first mixture, with milk if needed, and make a stiff dough. Knead slightly and roll one-fourth inch thick. Cut with a fancy cutter, brush over with beaten white of egg, and sprinkle with granulated sugar and chopped almonds. Bake on greased pans in a quick oven.

Rumford Doughnuts

1 quart flour.
½ teaspoon salt.
2 teaspoons Rumford Bak-
    ing Powder.

½ teaspoon ground nutmeg
    or cinnamon.
⅔ cup sugar
2 eggs.

About 1½ cups milk.

Sift together the flour, salt, baking powder and spice; add the sugar and mix to a soft dough with the eggs and milk. Cut out, fry in deep fat, drain, and sprinkle with sugar.

Puff Ball Doughnuts

3 eggs.
1 cup sugar.
1 pint milk.
½ teaspoon salt.

⅓ teaspoon nutmeg.
About 1 quart flour.
2 teaspoons Rumford Baking
    Powder.

Frying fat.

Beat the eggs and sugar till quite light, and add the milk, salt and nutmeg; sift the baking powder with two cups of the flour and add, beating well. Sift and add more flour till a thick, heavy batter is the result. Drop by spoonfuls into hot fat and cook about three minutes, turning twice that all sides may be evenly browned. Drain very thoroughly on unglazed paper.

Rye Drop Cakes

1 cup rye flour.	¾ cup milk.
1½ teaspoons Rumford	⅓ cup white flour.
Baking Powder.	1 egg.
1 tablespoon sugar.	Pinch of salt.

Sift all dry ingredients together and make a rather thick batter with the egg and milk. Dip a spoon into hot fat and take up the batter with it; drop by spoonfuls into deep fat and cook slowly about six minutes. The fat must not be as hot as for doughnuts or the cakes will brown before being thoroughly cooked through.

Wonders

1 egg.	¼ teaspoon salt.
	About ¾ cup flour.

Beat the egg, add salt and enough flour to make a stiff dough — about three-fourths cup will usually be sufficient. Roll out on a floured board till as thin as a wafer, and cut with a large round cutter. Drop separately into hot fat, fry golden brown, drain well and dust with powdered sugar.

Macaroons

½ pound almond paste.	⅔ cup powdered sugar.
Whites of 4 large eggs.	

Break up the almond paste with a fork, add the powdered sugar and mix till the paste is pulverized. Beat the whites of the eggs thoroughly and mix with the almond paste and sugar. Drop by teaspoonfuls on greased paper spread on baking pans, and bake about twenty minutes in a moderate oven.

German Macaroons

½ pound brown sugar.   3 egg whites.
½ pound ground almonds.   Juice of half a lemon.
Wafer paper.

Put the whites of eggs in a bowl, and stir in the
sugar slowly; strain and add the lemon juice, and
put in the almonds, a little at a time. Mix smoothly
and drop by teaspoonfuls about two inches apart on
the wafer paper which has been laid on baking-tins.
Bake in a very slow oven till golden brown.

Oatmeal Macaroons

1 tablespoon butter.   2½ cups rolled oats.
1 cup granulated sugar.   1 teaspoon Rumford Baking
2 eggs.   Powder.
¼ teaspoon salt.

Soften the butter slightly, add the sugar, then the
beaten eggs, next the oats, baking powder and salt
mixed together. Drop by spoonfuls on greased pans,
and bake about twelve minutes in a hot oven.

MEMORANDA

MEMORANDA

ICE CREAM AND ICES

GENERAL DIRECTIONS FOR FREEZING

TO insure good frozen desserts it is necessary to use the best ingredients, the ice and salt in the right proportions and to freeze at the proper rate of speed.

Always boil sugar and water together to a syrup for water ices, as this melts the sugar thoroughly and gives body to the ices.

When cream is the foundation for the dessert, scald it, and add the sugar to the scalding cream.

When a custard is used as the base of the frozen mixture, cook eggs and milk in a double boiler. Do not add flavoring till all ingredients are quite cold, as extracts are volatile and lose much of their strength if added to a hot mixture.

Genuine Philadelphia Ice Cream is made from sweetened and flavored pure cream without the addition of eggs or any thickening medium.

French Ice Cream has a rich custard as its base.

Punch is a water ice with cordial or other liquor added.

Sherbet is a water ice without the addition of whites of eggs.

Mousse and **Parfait** are cream mixtures frozen without stirring.

Have the liquid perfectly cold when put into the freezer.

When fruit is used do not add it till the mixture is about half frozen; also be sure that all fruit is thoroughly mashed, or it will freeze too hard. Use about one cup of fruit, nuts or macaroons to one quart of cream, and allow room for the cream to expand — one and one-half pints being sufficient for a quart freezer.

171

Crush the ice and mix with the salt before packing it around the freezer can.

For Ice Cream use one part of salt to three parts of ice by measure.

For Mousses and Parfaits, which are not stirred, equal measures of ice and salt should be used, as is also the case when previously frozen mixtures are being moulded.

For Water Ices two parts of ice to one of salt will give the best results.

In the preparation of ice cream, after the freezer can is in place, filled, and the ice and salt packed around it, let the mixture stand about five minutes; then turn the crank steadily, but not too fast, for the first few moments, afterwards increasing the speed till the freezing is completed. Then remove the dasher and scrape the mixture from the sides of the can, packing it down firmly. Replace the top on the can and cover with more ice. Put a piece of carpet or other heavy material over all, and stand aside for the mixture to ripen.

Vanilla Ice Cream

1 pint milk.	2 teaspoons vanilla extract.
3 eggs.	⅓ teaspoon salt.
1 cup sugar.	2 cups thin cream.

Scald the milk, add the well-beaten eggs to it and cook in a double boiler till as thick as boiled custard. Remove from the fire, add the sugar and, when cold, the vanilla, salt and cream. Freeze, and set aside to ripen before serving.

Various additions and flavorings may be added to this which may be called a "stock cream"; for example, two squares of chocolate melted over hot water may be added to the scalded milk before the eggs are put in, to give chocolate cream; or one-half cup of coffee may be scalded with the milk and the grounds afterwards removed by straining, the eggs added and the cream frozen as usual, for coffee ice cream. Crystallized cherries or ginger may be cut in small pieces and added to the cream when it is half frozen, when it will be known by the name of the fruit added.

Brown Bread Ice Cream

This cream may be made by the previous rule, adding one cup of brown bread crumbs, dried and crushed, to the cream just before putting it into the freezer.

Chocolate Ice Cream

1 quart thin cream.	½ teaspoon salt.
1 cup sugar.	2 squares unsweetened baking chocolate.
2 teaspoons vanilla extract	

Scald the cream, add the sugar and let it melt, and when the cream is cold add the extract, salt and the chocolate, the latter melted by placing it in a cup over boiling water. Stir well to blend the ingredients thoroughly, freeze and stand aside to ripen.

If preferred, the chocolate when melted may be added to the cream while the latter is hot; but the vanilla must be left out till just before freezing as the flavor would be lost if added to the hot mixture.

Philadelphia Ice Cream

1 quart thin cream.	1 cup sugar.
	Flavoring.

Scald the cream, without actually boiling it; add the sugar and, when cold, the flavoring. Freeze, turning the dasher steadily but not too fast. When set, remove the dasher, pack the cream down and put aside to ripen.

Peach Ice Cream

1 pint milk.	2 cups peach pulp.
1 cup heavy cream.	⅓ teaspoon almond extract.
1½ cups sugar.	

Scald the milk and cream, add the sugar and allow the mixture to cool; put in the flavoring and half

freeze, then add the peach pulp and finish freezing.
Remove the dasher, pack the cream down and cover
closely.   Set aside to ripen before serving.

Burnt Almond Ice Cream

1 cup cream.	1 cup sugar.
2 cups milk.	1 cup almonds.
4 egg yolks.	⅓ teaspoon almond extract.

⅓ cup sugar.

Scald the cream and milk and pour over the yolks
of eggs and one cup of the sugar; cook in a double
boiler till the mixture will coat the back of a spoon.
Set aside to cool while the almonds are being prepared.

Melt the remaining one-third cup sugar in a frying-
pan over a gentle heat, and cook till it forms a
caramel.   Blanch and chop the almonds finely, add
them to the caramel, and brown.   Cool till hard, then
pound finely and add with the extract to the custard.
Freeze and set aside to ripen.

Frozen Custard

1 quart milk.	1 cup sugar.
6 egg yolks.	1 cup cream.

1 teaspoon vanilla extract.

Scald the milk and pour it over the yolks of eggs
previously beaten with the sugar.   Turn into the
inner vessel of a double boiler and cook over hot
water till the custard coats the back of a spoon.
Strain, and when cold add cream and flavoring.
Freeze and stand aside to ripen before serving.

Nesselrode Pudding

1 cup mashed chestnuts.	⅓ cup water.
1 cup raisins.	4 egg yolks.
⅓ cup canned peaches.	1 pint cream.
⅓ cup crystallized cherries.	1 teaspoon vanilla extract.
1 cup sugar.	⅓ teaspoon almond extract.

Seed the raisins and cut up the peaches and cherries.
Boil the water and sugar together and when they have

cooked five minutes pour them over the beaten yolks of the eggs, beating while pouring; cook in a double boiler till as thick as boiled custard, strain and stand aside till cold. Add the flavoring, cream whipped till stiff, and the nuts. Turn into the freezer and, when beginning to stiffen, add the fruit. Finish freezing, pack in a mould and bury in ice for two hours.

Milk Sherbet

1 quart milk.	Grated rind of 1 lemon and
1½ cups sugar.	juice of 2.

Add the sugar to the milk and stir till dissolved, turn into the freezer and freeze till just beginning to set; then add the juice and rind of the lemons, and finish freezing.

Raspberry Sherbet

1 pint raspberry juice.	2 cups sugar.
1 quart water.	Juice of 2 lemons.

Crush and heat the raspberries so that the juice may be extracted more easily; pass through a fine sieve or cheese cloth to keep back the seeds. Boil the sugar and half the water to form a syrup, add the remainder of the water, the raspberry and lemon juice. Freeze as soon as the mixture is cold and, if possible, stand aside for an hour or more to ripen.

Orange Water Ice

1 pint water.	3 egg whites .
1 cup sugar.	Grated rind and juice of
2 teaspoons granulated	2 oranges.
gelatine.	Juice of 1 large lemon.

Boil the water and sugar together for ten minutes; add the gelatine, which has been previously softened in two tablespoons of cold water, and allow the mixture to become quite cold; then add the beaten whites of the eggs, the orange rind and juice and the lemon juice. Freeze, turning the dasher slowly but steadily, and when set, remove the dasher, pack the ice down solidly in the can, cover and put aside to ripen.

Coffee Parfait

1 cup sugar.	3 egg whites.
1 cup water.	1 cup strong coffee.

2 cups whipped cream.

Cook the sugar and water till they form a thick syrup; beat the whites of the eggs and pour the boiling syrup over them. Cool, add the coffee and, when quite cold, the whipped cream. Mix all well and put the mixture into a mould, cover very closely, and bury in ice and salt for several hours.

Roman Punch

1 quart water.	Juice of 2 lemons.
1½ cups sugar.	½ cup rum.

Boil the sugar and water till the sugar is dissolved; remove from the fire and, when cold, add the lemon juice. Partly freeze and, when beginning to thicken, add the rum and finish freezing. Let the punch ripen at least two hours before serving.

MEMORANDA

MEMORANDA

CANNING, PRESERVING AND PICKLING

THE chief difference between canning and preserving is in the amount of sugar used. In canning, from one-fourth to one-third is the most common quantity; while in jelly making, from three-fourths to equal parts may be required, according to the acidity of the fruit.

Canning is the more economical method, and possesses the advantage of retaining more nearly the fresh flavor of the fruit. With many housekeepers the chances that a jar of fruit will keep perfectly, or that it will spoil, are about even. Many consider it a question of luck, but if fruit is cooked thoroughly, placed in sterilized jars and properly sealed, it must keep, and can neither mould nor ferment. The jars must be free from cracks and used for no other purpose than canning fruit. The rubbers must be new, and sterilized at the same time as the jars; it is not economy to use old rubbers.

To insure success three rules must be followed:

1. All fruit used, while ripe, must not be over-ripe nor at all soft.

2. Absolute cleanliness must be observed in everything used for cooking and storing the fruit: have all jars, covers, rubbers, spoons, etc., sterilized immediately before using.

3. Cover all jars or glasses while the contents are still scalding hot, so that no spores of mould may reach the fruit. In the case of jellies, if not convenient to seal them at once, cover with sheets of glass while cooling.

To sterilize utensils and receptacles used in jelly making and canning, wash thoroughly and place in a pan, cover with cold water and bring to a fast boil. Fill each jar or glass as removed from the boiling water without allowing time to cool.

Jelly bags may be made of cheese cloth, muslin or flannel. Before using, wet with cold water, other-

179

wise some juice will be absorbed by the bag and wasted.

Canned fruits are richer if cooked in a syrup instead of in water to which sugar is added to form a syrup after the fruit is cooked.

TO PREPARE SYRUPS FOR CANNED FRUITS

For Plums, Peaches, Cherries, Pears, Blackberries and other sweet varieties of fruits, use one pound of sugar to a quart of water.

For the more acid fruits, such as currants, sour cherries, etc., use one pound of sugar to a pint and a half of water. The longer the sugar and water are cooked together the heavier the syrup will be. Cook without stirring, to prevent crystallizing.

As a general rule fifteen minutes cooking after reaching boiling point will be sufficient to sterilize fruits, with the exception of very seedy ones, such as currants, which will take a little longer owing to the viscous nature of the substance surrounding the seeds.

The Selection of Fruit. Be sure that it has been freshly gathered on a dry day and is not over-ripe. The finest flavor does not develop till the fruit ripens, but the pectin, which is the jellying principle, loses some of its properties immediately after this stage; therefore, use fruit that is rather under than over ripe, especially for jellies and preserves.

When washing is necessary place the fruit, a little at a time, in a colander and run water gently through and over it, draining well afterwards. Peaches can be pared without waste by dipping a few at a time in boiling water and removing the skin with a sharp knife, as one would remove the skin from a tomato.

To Can Fruit in Jars over the Fire. Fill the jars with prepared fruit and place in a steamer or other large vessel containing warm water. The jars must be protected from the bottom and sides of the

vessel and from each other, either by putting them
in a rack made for the purpose, or by placing hay,
excelsior or paper under and around them. Put on
the covers but do not screw them down. Let the
water come within four inches of the top of the jars,
and cover the cooking vessel to prevent the escape
of steam. Cook for fifteen minutes after reaching
boiling point; take out the jars, one at a time, fill
with boiling syrup, seal and cool. Tighten the covers when the fruit is cold.

To Can by the Open Kettle Process. Make a
syrup of any desired sweetness. If a very rich flavor
is wanted make the syrup from sugar and extra fruit
juice instead of sugar and water. Prepare the fruit,
cook it in the syrup till tender, and then fill and seal
the sterilized jars as usual. It is the sterilizing, not
the quantity of sugar used, that insures the keeping
of fruit.

To Can without Cooking. This method is suitable for sour fruits such as rhubarb and gooseberries.
Cut the former into two-inch lengths; top and tail
the latter. Fill the jars with the fruit and run cold
water from the faucet into them for ten minutes.
Seal as usual. The natural acid of the fruit will keep
it without cooking.

Always examine the jars carefully before putting
away, and be sure the covers are screwed as tightly
as possible. It is a wise precaution to turn each
jar upside down for a short time.

As all canned fruits keep better in a dark, cool
place, an excellent plan is to put each jar into a
red or blue paper bag which protects it from light.

JELLY MAKING

All fruits for jelly making should be gathered just
before they are fully ripe and on a dry day. Acid
fruits are most suitable as they contain more pectin
— the jellying principle — than the sweeter varieties.

Strawberries and blackberries are difficult to make jelly from without the addition of some other fruit, such as apple, currants, etc.

Currant and Grape Jellies. Pick over the fruit carefully and remove all foreign matter; put in a preserving kettle and crush to liberate the juice, heat till it flows freely, then place in a jelly bag previously wrung out of cold water, and let the juice drip slowly. It may be left to drip over night. Measure, heat to boiling point, add the heated sugar — pound to pint — and boil five minutes; skim if necessary, test and, if it jellies, pour at once into glasses. Cover according to any of the directions given later.

If a light, delicate color is desired in making currant jelly, the stalks must be removed. This takes time, but the result warrants it.

In some cases good jelly can be made by using only three-fourths of a pint of sugar to a pint of juice. This applies to fruits which contain a large proportion of sugar in themselves and also when the season is exceptionally dry and sunny.

Apple, Plum, Crab-Apple or Quince Jelly. Wash, wipe and stem, and from apples, crab-apples and quinces remove the blossom; quinces need hard rubbing to remove the fuzz; from plums remove the stones. Cut all fruits into convenient-sized pieces, using a silver knife to prevent discoloration, and add water — for apples and crab-apples half as much water as fruit; for the other kinds of fruit use a little less water as they have more juice of their own. Cook until tender and strain through a jelly bag. Measure the juice and add the sugar, pound to pint, unless the fruit is very sweet, when a little less should be used; cook till the juice jellies when a little is cooled in a saucer; then put into glasses, and cover. It must be remembered that too long boiling destroys the jellying principle; consequently the fruit must not be allowed to cook longer than necessary.

If the sugar is heated after measuring, the jelly will be clearer and jell more quickly. The heating can be done while the fruit juice is coming to the boiling point. Jellies made by the Cold Process are the most delicate, but are not likely to keep quite as well as when fruit juice and sugar are cooked together. The method followed is the same as for ordinary jelly so far as the cooking, straining and measuring of the fruit and juice are concerned. The sugar—pound for pint—is added to the strained juice and dissolved; the sterilized glasses filled, and covered with sheets of glass to keep out the dust and attract the rays of the sun, and the jellies left in a sunny place till set. They are then covered according to directions given.

TO COVER JELLIES

There are three methods in common use:

1. Dip a round of paper in either alcohol or brandy, lay it on top of the jelly as soon as it is cold and then put the tin cover of the glass over the top.

2. Dip a round of paper in slightly-beaten white of egg, cover the glass with this and press down till the paper adheres closely. The paper must be large enough to overlap the top of the glass at least half an inch on all sides.

3. Cover the jelly, when cold, with melted paraffine wax, having the wax quarter of an inch thick as it contracts when cold, and if too thin a portion of the jelly will be left uncovered.

Preserved Rhubarb

6 pounds rhubarb.	Rind of 1 lemon, or 1 ounce
4 pounds sugar.	whole ginger, if desired.

Make a syrup of the sugar with just enough water to prevent burning and add the lemon, or ginger if used. Cut the rhubarb into two-inch lengths and cook in the syrup gently to prevent breaking. It is better to cook a small quantity at a time. Place the fruit in jars as soon as tender; boil the syrup rapidly till it is thick, pour over the fruit, and seal.

Spiced Grapes

8 pounds grapes.	4 sticks cinnamon.
4 pounds sugar.	1 ounce whole cloves.
3 cups vinegar.	2 blades mace.

Remove and set aside the skins of the grapes; cook the pulp in the vinegar with the spices tied in cheese cloth, till the grapes are soft. Pass as much as possible through a fine sieve, keeping back the seeds. Add the skins and return to the fire; when boiling put in the sugar and bag of spices. Cook till thick and then put into glasses and seal.

Ginger Pears

½ pound green ginger, scraped and chopped.	8 pounds sugar. 1 pint water.
Juice and shredded peel of 4 oranges and 3 lemons.	8 pounds pears weighed after paring and coring.

Cook the ginger, orange and lemon peel with a pint of water till tender; then add the sugar, orange and lemon juice; cook till the sugar is dissolved; put in the pears chopped coarsely, and cook very slowly for two hours. Put into small jars and cover when cold. The green ginger may be tied in a bag if preferred, and removed after the cooking is completed.

Brandied Figs

4 pounds figs.	2 cups water.
4 pounds sugar.	2 inches vanilla bean.
Brandy.	

Wash, soak and steam the figs for twenty minutes. Make a syrup by boiling together the sugar and water, and when the sugar is dissolved add the figs and cook till they are transparent. Set aside for twenty-four hours; then drain off the liquid, boil it down till very thick and add the vanilla bean to it while cooking. When cold remove the vanilla, and measure and add an equal quantity of the best French brandy. Put the figs in bottles or jars, fill to overflowing with the syrup, and seal at once.

Gooseberry Jelly

3 quarts of green goose-   2 quarts water.
   berries.   Sugar.

Wash the gooseberries, put them in a preserving kettle with the water and cook over a slow fire till the berries are soft enough to mash easily; strain, and press through a jelly bag, and to every pint of juice add one pound sugar. Cook rapidly for ten minutes, skimming well while boiling. Turn into glasses, and seal when cold.

Orange Marmalade

1 dozen oranges.   Water.
1½ pounds sugar to each   If the oranges are sweet, 1
   pound of fruit.   lemon to each 4 oranges.

If possible procure the bitter Seville oranges, or, if these are not obtainable, use lemons in the proportion named.

Wash the fruit and cut into the thinnest possible slices, cover with cold water, using one pint of water to each pound of fruit and set aside over night. In the morning bring to the boiling point and cook very slowly till the skins are sufficiently tender to be easily pierced by the head of a pin. When cold weigh again and add one and one-half pounds of sugar for every pound of fruit and juice, and cook till thick and transparent. Put in glasses, and seal when cold.

Lemon Marmalade

1 dozen lemons.   Water.
1½ pounds sugar to each pound of fruit and water.

Choose smooth, thin-skinned lemons, cut into very thin slices, remove and keep the seeds. Add a pint of water for each pound of fruit and stand aside over night. In the morning boil gently till the fruit is tender, and again set aside till cold. Weigh and add the sugar in the proportions named. Put the seeds in a bag and cook with the fruit. When the whole is thick and transparent put into glasses, and seal when cold.

Chopped Raw Pickle

2 quarts tomatoes.	⅔ cup salt.
⅔ cup grated horseradish.	½ cup mustard seeds.
2 large onions.	½ teaspoon each ground cin-
2 heads celery.	namon, cloves, ginger
2 red peppers.	and mace.
1 cup sugar.	1 quart vinegar.

Peel and chop the tomatoes, add the horseradish, then the onions, celery and peppers, all chopped. Mix well, and stir in the sugar, salt, mustard seeds and spices. Pour the vinegar over and mix thoroughly. Keep at least two weeks before using.

Green Tomato Pickle

½ bushel green tomatoes.	1 stick cinnamon.
¼ peck onions.	1 teaspoon ground mace.
2 cups salt.	¼ cup whole peppercorns.
9 green peppers.	2 tablespoons mustard.
1 teaspoon ground cloves.	5 pounds brown sugar.
	3 quarts vinegar.

Slice the onions and tomatoes, sprinkle the salt over them and stand over night. Drain and place in a large saucepan with the peppers from which the seeds have been removed, and then add the spices, sugar, mustard and vinegar and cook one hour. Seal when cold.

Mustard Pickle

24 small cucumbers.	½ pound mustard.
1 quart very small onions.	¼ ounce turmeric.
2 cauliflowers.	¾ cup flour.
2 quarts green tomatoes.	1 cup sugar.
6 green peppers.	3½ quarts vinegar.
	Salt.

Cut such of the vegetables as require it into very small pieces, adding those that are small enough without cutting, and stand them over night in brine sufficiently strong to float an egg. In the morning scald all together and drain thoroughly.

Mix the mustard, turmeric, flour and sugar to a smooth paste with one pint of the vinegar, and add to the three quarts of vinegar which has been brought to the boiling point. Cook twenty minutes, add the vegetables and, when cold, place in jars and seal.

Chili Sauce

2 dozen tomatoes.	2 tablespoons salt.
3 green peppers.	1 tablespoon each ground
3 onions.	cloves, nutmeg, ginger
¼ cup sugar.	and allspice.

1 quart vinegar.

Scald and peel the tomatoes, cut them in small pieces and put with all the other ingredients into a granite saucepan. Cook very slowly for three hours, and then bottle and seal.

Sweet Pickled Prunes

4 pounds prunes.	½ ounce cloves.
2 pounds sugar.	1 stick cinnamon.
2 cups vinegar.	½ ounce whole ginger.

Wash the prunes well, soak in cold water for twenty-four hours, and then bring them to the boiling point in the same water. Boil together the sugar, vinegar and spices for ten minutes; add the prunes, drained from the water, and simmer gently till tender. When cold, put in jars and seal closely.

Pickled Peaches

4 quarts peaches.	3 or 4 sticks cinnamon.
2 pounds sugar, prefer-	Cloves.
ably brown.	1½ pints vinegar.

Make a syrup with the sugar, vinegar and cinnamon, cooking them together for twenty minutes.

Remove the skin of the peaches by dipping them for a moment in boiling water, then rubbing with a cloth. Stick two cloves in each peach and then cook in the syrup till tender. Do not try to cook too many peaches at one time. Boil the syrup ten minutes after all the fruit is done, then pour it over the peaches, and seal.

Tomato Catsup

4 quarts sliced tomatoes.	1 quart vinegar.
8 green peppers.	2 tablespoons white pepper.
4 tablespoons salt.	3 tablespoons mustard.
1 tablespoon allspice.	

Cook the tomatoes and peppers in the salt and vinegar till tender. Rub through a sieve, passing through all the pulp possible; add the spices and seasonings, and boil all slowly for three hours. Bottle and seal when cold.

MEMORANDA

MEMORANDA

RECIPES FOR THE CHAFING-DISH

THE chafing-dish affords a means of preparing on the serving table, at the time of eating, small dishes which do not need very long cooking. Alcohol or gas may be employed as the fuel, but the former is generally used. Proof alcohol is best as it gives greater heat and burns longer than wood alcohol. All good chafing-dishes have two pans, the blazer and the hot-water pan. With dishes containing eggs, and those requiring slow cooking, use both pans. Such preparations as will not be harmed by close contact with the flame may be cooked without the water pan.

The lamp may be adjusted to give either a moderate or quick heat. In preparing to use a chafing-dish at table be sure that all ingredients, seasoning, etc., are at hand that no time may be wasted when the lamp is lighted. Have a tray under the dish in case water or alcohol overflows.

All dishes that can be cooked in a short time in a frying-pan or saucepan are suitable for the chafing-dish, and all recipes given under this heading can be cooked over the fire. Frying-pans, toasters and many accessories can be obtained for use with the chafing-dish.

Celeried Oysters

1 tablespoon butter.	1 tablespoon minced celery.
1 dozen large oysters.	Seasoning.
1 wineglass sherry.	

Melt the butter, add the oysters and celery, cook three minutes, add seasoning and sherry, and serve very hot on buttered toast.

191

Epicurean Oysters

1 pint solid oysters.	⅓ teaspoon celery salt.
3 tablespoons butter.	Pepper or cayenne to taste.
½ cup cream.	2 tablespoons sherry.

Pick over the oysters carefully and cook them three minutes with the butter; add the cream, celery salt and pepper, and bring to the boiling point. Put in the sherry at the moment of serving, and pour over hot toast.

Oysters with Mushrooms

2 cups oysters.	Salt, pepper and lemon juice
3 tablespoons butter.	to taste.
3 large mushrooms.	1 egg yolk.
2 tablespoons flour.	2 tablespoons sherry.

Scald the oysters and drain the liquor from them; melt the butter, chop the mushrooms and cook them in the butter for three minutes; add the flour, then the oyster liquor, stirring constantly and, when boiling, add the seasoning. Put in and heat the oysters and, lastly, add the egg and wine. Serve very hot on toast.

Oysters à la Poulette

3 tablespoons butter.	½ cup thin cream.
3 tablespoons flour.	1 pint solid oysters.
1 cup milk.	1 teaspoon lemon juice.

Put the butter and flour in the chafing-dish, and cook till they are smoothly blended. Add the milk a little at a time, stirring constantly till the sauce boils; put in the cream and again stir till boiling point is reached. Pick over the oysters and free them from shell, heat in the sauce and, just before serving, add the lemon juice.

Pigs in Blankets

1 dozen large oysters.	1 dozen thin slices of bacon.

Seasoning.

Pick over the oysters carefully, roll each in a slice of bacon and fasten the ends with a skewer. Put in a hot chafing-dish and cook till the bacon is crisp. Season, and serve very hot.

Minced Clams

25 clams.	2 tablespoons chopped
4 tablespoons melted	parsley.
butter.	Salt, pepper and lemon juice.
⅔ cup clam liquor.	

Open and mince the clams, saving all the liquor. Melt the butter, add the minced clams and liquor, cook three minutes and put in the parsley and lemon juice. Heat thoroughly, season, and serve on toast.

Fricasseed Clams

2 tablespoons butter.	⅓ cup cream.
1½ tablespoons flour.	1½ dozen clams.
1 cup clam juice.	2 egg yolks.
¼ cup sherry.	

Melt the butter, add the flour and, when these are smooth, the clam juice; next the cream and, as soon as the sauce boils, the clams coarsely chopped. Cook three minutes, and then add the egg yolks and sherry. Serve on toast.

Deviled Lobster

2 tablespoons butter.	1 teaspoon lemon juice.
1 tablespoon dry mustard.	Meat of 1 lobster.
½ teaspoon salt.	⅓ cup butter.
1 tablespoon Worcestershire or tomato sauce.	

Beat the two tablespoons of butter to a cream; add the mustard, salt, sauce and lemon juice. Cut the lobster in neat pieces, sauté for about six minutes in the remaining butter and, when nearly done, add the creamed mixture. Heat the whole thoroughly, and serve on toast.

Lobster à la Newburg

2 pounds lobster.	Grating of nutmeg.
½ cup butter.	¼ cup thin cream.
¼ teaspoon salt.	3 egg yolks.
Few grains cayenne.	1 tablespoon sherry.

Remove the lobster meat from the shell and cut in small pieces. Melt the butter, add the lobster and cook three minutes. Put in the seasonings, next the cream and, when this is hot, yolks of the eggs slightly beaten. Stir till thick, add the sherry and serve very hot.

Shrimps à la Creole

2 tablespoons butter.	1½ cups stewed, strained
1 teaspoon onion juice or	tomato.
grated onion.	1 bay leaf.
1½ tablespoons flour.	Salt and pepper to taste.
1 can or 1 pint shrimps.	

Melt the butter, put in the onion juice and flour and stir till smooth; add the seasonings, tomato and bay leaf, and stir constantly till boiling. Pick over the shrimps and heat them in the sauce. Serve plain or with boiled rice.

Deviled Eggs

2 tablespoons butter.	¼ teaspoon paprika or
1 teaspoon dry mustard.	pepper.
2 tablespoons tomato	⅓ teaspoon salt.
catsup.	6 hard-cooked eggs.
2 tablespoons Worcestershire sauce.	

Put together in the chafing-dish and heat all the ingredients, except the eggs. Bring to the boiling point and add the eggs cut in slices. Heat, and serve on hot buttered toast.

Scrambled Eggs with Tomatoes

2 tablespoons butter.	1 cup canned or stewed
1 teaspoon minced onion.	tomato.
	Salt and pepper to taste.

6 eggs.

Melt the butter and cook the onion in it for two minutes; add the tomato and seasonings and then the eggs slightly beaten. Cook till creamy, and serve on toast.

Eggs with Green Peppers

2 tablespoons butter.	1 tablespoon tomato catsup.
4 finely-minced green	6 eggs beaten with ¼ cup
peppers.	cream.

2 tablespoons grated cheese.

Cook all the ingredients, except the eggs and cream, two minutes; then add eggs and stir till thick. Serve on toast.

Welsh Rabbit

1½ pounds cheese.	1 teaspoon dry mustard.
1 tablespoon butter.	⅓ teaspoon pepper or a little
¼ cup ale or milk.	less of cayenne.
1 tablespoon Worcester-	1 egg.
shire sauce.	

Cut the cheese into small pieces and put it in the upper part of the chafing-dish, having water in the lower pan. Let the cheese melt and become creamy, add the butter, ale (or milk) and seasonings; cook till smooth and, just before serving, stir in the egg slightly beaten. This prevents the rabbit being stringy. Have ready slices of bread or toast (preferably the former), dip them into the cheese and pour more over them on the serving plate.

Savory Rabbit

6 slices bread.	4 ounces grated cheese.
Butter.	2 tablespoons ale or thin
Minced ham or anchovy	cream.
paste.	Seasoning to taste.

Cut the bread into round or square slices and sauté in the butter till slightly crisped. The quantity of butter will depend on the freshness of the bread, as the fresher it is the more butter it will absorb. Spread each piece with the ham or anchovy and keep hot. Melt the cheese in the blazer of the chafing-dish, and add the ale and seasoning. Spread over the ham and serve immediately.

Blushing Bunny

1½ pounds cheese.
1 tablespoon butter.
1 cup cooked, strained
    tomato, or canned
    tomato soup.

⅓ teaspoon mustard.
⅓ teaspoon pepper.
1 teaspoon lemon juice.

Melt the cheese as for Welsh Rabbit; add the butter and tomato, stirring constantly; season to taste, and add the lemon juice just before serving.

Cheese Fondue

1 tablespoon butter.
1 cup milk.
1 cup bread crumbs.

2 cups grated mild cheese.
1 teaspoon dry mustard.
Cayenne.

2 eggs.

Melt the butter in the chafing-dish; add the milk, bread crumbs, cheese and mustard, and season with cayenne. Stir constantly and add two lightly-beaten eggs a moment before serving.

Cheese Toast Sandwiches

¾ cup grated cheese.
1 tablespoon cream.
½ teaspoon dry mustard.

A little cayenne.
Rounds of bread.
⅓ cup butter.

Put the cheese in a bowl with the cream and seasonings, adding more cream if necessary to form a paste. Spread this between the slices of bread, and press closely together. Sauté on both sides in the butter melted in the blazer of the chafing-dish.

Chicken Livers Sautéd

3 tablespoons butter, or   2 tablespoons flour.
    butter and bacon fat.   1 cup stock.
6 livers.   1 teaspoon lemon juice.
1 teaspoon onion juice.   Seasoning.

Melt the butter and cook the livers and onion juice
in it for three minutes; add the flour, stir smoothly,
and pour in the stock; bring to the boiling point and
cook two minutes. Season, and serve at once or the
livers will become tough.

Lamb Terrapin

2 cups cold lamb cut into   1 tablespoon Worcestershire
    dice.   sauce.
2 tablespoons butter.   1 cup stock.
1 teaspoon dry mustard.   ¼ cup cream.
1 tablespoon flour.   2 hard-cooked eggs.
        2 tablespoons sherry.

Remove superfluous fat from the lamb. Melt the
butter and add to it the mustard, flour and, when
these are smoothly mixed, the stock, cream and sauce.
Cook five minutes after the sauce reaches boiling
point. Put in the meat, and yolks of the eggs passed
through a sieve. Heat, and then stir in whites of
the eggs finely chopped, and the sherry. Season,
and serve on toast.

Sweetbreads with Peas

2 tablespoons butter.   ½ cup cream.
1½ tablespoons flour.   2 sweetbreads.
1 cup milk.   1 cup French peas.
        Seasoning to taste.

Melt the butter, add the flour and stir till smooth.
Add the milk and cream gradually, stirring constantly till boiling. Have the sweetbreads previously cooked and cut into large cubes, add to the
sauce with the peas and seasoning, and heat
thoroughly.

Deviled Tomatoes

4 firm tomatoes.	2 teaspoons sugar.
⅓ cup butter.	1 teaspoon mustard.
Seasoning of salt and	1 whole egg.
pepper.	1 hard-cooked egg yolk.
4 tablespoons butter.	¼ cup vinegar.

Peel and slice the tomatoes, season, and cook in the butter till tender. Keep hot while the sauce is being prepared. Cream the butter, sugar and mustard; add the hard-cooked and raw eggs, then the vinegar and seasoning. Cook in the upper pan, over hot water, till thick. Pour over the tomatoes, and serve hot.

MEMORANDA

MEMORANDA

SANDWICHES

BREAD for sandwiches should be not less than twelve hours old, rather close grained and of such shape as to cut without waste, the regular sandwich loaves being the best for the purpose. The butter should be sufficiently soft to spread easily, and is better creamed as for cake. Seasonings can be sometimes beaten into the butter, thus saving labor in spreading. The bread may be spread with butter either before or after cutting from the loaf. Be sure that the slices are kept in the order of slicing that they may fit together after filling.

Cheese and Green Pepper Sandwiches

½ pound cheese.   Salt.
3 green peppers.   Slices of bread.

Remove the seeds and white pith and pass the peppers through a meat chopper with the cheese, season to taste, and mix smoothly. The juice from the peppers will moisten the cheese sufficiently for it to spread easily. Have the bread cut rather thicker than usual for sandwiches. Spread the cheese paste rather thickly on one slice of bread and cover with another; press together firmly and toast over a hot fire. Cut into strips and tuck between the folds of a napkin to keep them hot.

Monaco Sandwiches

Yolks of 2 hard-cooked   2 tablespoons salmon or
  eggs.   shrimp paste.
3 tablespoons butter.   2 tablespoons butter.
Pepper to taste.   Unbuttered Graham or
                                brown bread.

Put the yolks of eggs into a bowl with the butter and rub with the back of a spoon till smooth. Add the pepper and fish paste and, when these are blended, the butter. Spread rather thickly between slices of bread and cut off the crusts.

Ham and Egg Sandwiches

Thin slices of buttered white bread.	1 tablespoon mayonnaise or cream dressing to each egg.
Hard-cooked eggs.	
1 tablespoon minced ham to each egg.	Salt and pepper to taste.

Have the eggs finely chopped or pass them through a meat chopper; add the ham, dressing and seasoning, and mix well. Spread the mixture on a slice of buttered bread and cover with another. Trim off the crusts and cut into diamonds or triangles.

Boston Sandwiches

Slices of thinly cut Boston brown bread.	½ cup peanuts.
	1 teaspoon lemon juice.
2 rolls Neufchatel cheese.	2 tablespoons cream.
6 stoned olives.	Salt and pepper.

Mash the cheese smoothly, add the olives chopped small, the peanuts passed through a meat chopper (peanut butter may be substituted), the lemon juice, cream and seasoning. Spread thickly on the brown bread and press two slices together.

Savory Sandwiches

3 tablespoons butter.	2 teaspoons chopped parsley.
1 teaspoon capers.	
6 olives.	A few drops of onion juice.
1 tablespoon chopped mustard pickle.	Slices of buttered white or Graham bread.

Beat the butter to a cream, add the capers and olives chopped finely; mix these well with the butter and stir in the pickle, parsley and onion juice, with salt if necessary. Spread between slices of either white or Graham bread, well buttered.

Cheese Butter Sandwiches

½ cup butter.
6 tablespoons dry, sharp-flavored cheese.
1 teaspoon made mustard.

1 teaspoon anchovy paste or sauce.
2 teaspoons Worcestershire sauce.

Slices of buttered bread.

Beat the butter to a cream, add the cheese (grated), the mustard, anchovy and Worcestershire sauces. Beat till well blended, and spread between slices of buttered bread.

Cucumber Sandwiches

2 cucumbers.
1 teaspoon onion juice.

⅓ cup mayonnaise.
Salt and pepper.

Slices of buttered bread.

Peel the cucumbers and remove the seeds if coarse; chop the cucumbers finely and place them in a cloth or a sieve to drain. To the drained pulp add the onion juice, seasoning and mayonnaise. Spread between slices of buttered whole wheat or Graham bread.

Nut and Raisin Sandwiches

1½ cups seeded raisins.
½ cup chopped nuts.

Juice of half a lemon.
Buttered Graham or white bread.

Chop the raisins finely or pass them through a meat chopper with the shelled nuts; blend smoothly and moisten with the lemon juice. Spread between slices of well-buttered bread.

Club Sandwich

Toasted bread.	Slices of tomato.
Slices of bacon.	Lettuce.
White meat of chicken.	Mayonnaise dressing.

Butter lightly a slice of toast and lay on it slices of bacon cut very thin and well broiled. Over this place slices of the white meat of chicken, then tomato, lettuce and a good portion of mayonnaise. Lay another slice of buttered toast over the top and serve at once.

Sweet Chocolate Sandwiches

2 squares chocolate.	⅓ cup shelled and finely-
1 cup pulverized sugar.	chopped nuts.
2 tablespoons butter.	3 tablespoons cream.
Slices of buttered white bread.	

Melt the chocolate over a gentle heat, add the butter, sugar and cream, and cook five minutes over hot water; add the nuts and mix. Cool slightly before spreading between the slices of buttered bread.

MEMORANDA

MEMORANDA

CONFECTIONS

Molasses Candy

2 cups molasses.   2 tablespoons butter.
2 cups brown sugar.   ½ cup water.
¼ cup vinegar.

Put all the ingredients, except the vinegar, into a large saucepan and cook fast till a little of the mixture dropped into cold water feels brittle; add the vinegar, cook two minutes more and pour into a greased pan to cool. As soon as it can be easily handled, pull with the fingers till white. Cut into pieces before it is too hard.

Maple Kisses

2 cups maple sugar.   ¼ cup butter.
¾ cup water.   1 cup shelled pecan nuts.

Cook the water, sugar and butter till a little dropped in cold water forms a firm ball; add the nuts, stir till the mixture begins to cool and thicken, and then drop, in small spoonfuls, on a greased paper or plate.

Peanut Brittle

2 cups granulated sugar.   1 teaspoon butter.
1 cup coarsely-chopped peanuts.

Put the sugar into an iron saucepan and let it melt over a moderately hot fire; add the butter and nuts and immediately pour into a well-greased pan. Mark into squares when sufficiently cool.

Peppermint Drops

1 cup granulated sugar.   ¼ cup water.
6 drops essence of peppermint.

Cook the water and sugar till a little lifted on a fork or spoon spins a thread. Do not stir while cooking. Remove from the fire, add the peppermint and stir till the candy thickens and looks cloudy. Drop immediately from a teaspoon on a greased paper or plate. If it becomes too hard to drop, warm by standing the saucepan over hot water for a moment.

Wintergreen drops may be made by the same rule, substituting wintergreen for the peppermint.

Dakota Caramels

2 cups brown sugar.	⅓ cup butter.
1 cup molasses.	1 cup milk.
¼ pound grated chocolate.	1 cup shelled, chopped nuts.

Put all ingredients, except the nuts, into a large saucepan, cook twenty minutes over a gentle heat and then test by dropping a little of the mixture into cold water. If it forms a firm ball remove from the fire, add the chopped nuts and pour into a greased tin. Cut into squares when nearly cold.

Fudge

2 cups sugar.	¾ cup milk.
1 tablespoon butter.	1 square (1 ounce) chocolate.

Cook all together till a little dropped in cold water forms a soft ball; remove from the fire, beat well and pour into buttered pans. Cut into squares when nearly cold.

Chocolate Creams

1 egg white.	6 drops any desired flavor-
2 tablespoons cold water.	ing.
Confectioners' sugar.	¼ pound sweet chocolate.

Beat the egg and water together only till mixed; add the sugar till the ingredients form a stiff paste — about a cup and a half will probably be needed. Work in the flavoring with the sugar, then form into small balls. Grate the chocolate and put in a cup over hot water to melt; dip the balls into it, one at a time, using a fork for the dipping. Lay separately on waxed paper and, if necessary, dip a second time.

Creamed Walnuts

2 cups granulated sugar.	½ cup water.
Vanilla or other extract.	Shelled walnuts.

Cook the sugar and water, without stirring, till a little lifted from the pan on a fork will form a thread.

Cool quickly and then add flavoring, and beat with a spoon till white and creamy. Make this cream into small balls with the fingers; press half a shelled English walnut in each side and roll in fine granulated sugar; or dip each candy very gently in glacé sugar.

Glacé Sugar

2 cups granulated sugar. ⅛ teaspoon cream of tartar.
⅔ cup boiling water.

Boil the sugar, water and cream of tartar together till a little dropped in cold water is quite brittle and clear. Do not stir while cooking. If the sugar becomes too hard, add a tablespoon of water and cook and test again. Dip the prepared nuts in the hot syrup, one at a time, using a candy dipper or sugar tongs, being careful not to shake or stir the syrup. Lay the nuts, after dipping, on a greased paper or plate to harden.

Cocoanut Cream Candy

1 cocoanut. 1½ pounds granulated sugar.

Put the sugar and milk of the cocoanut together in a saucepan and cook five minutes; add the cocoanut and cook ten minutes longer, stirring constantly to prevent burning. Pour into greased pans and cool. Cut in squares and leave in a cool place two days to harden.

French Nougat

½ pound confectioners' ½ pound shelled almonds.
sugar.

Put the sugar into a shallow pan — preferably an iron one — melt it very slowly, stirring constantly. Chop the almonds finely and add to the melted sugar. Pour into well-greased pans to cool, cut in squares when almost cold and, if desired, dip the squares in melted chocolate.

Butter Scotch

2 cups sugar.   2 tablespoons water.
A piece of butter the size of an egg.

Put all together in a saucepan and cook, without stirring, till a little dropped in cold water is hard and brittle. Pour onto well-greased plates and, when nearly cold, mark into squares.

Pralines

2 cups confectioners' sugar.   1 cup maple syrup.
½ cup cream.   2 cups nut meats.

Boil the sugar, maple syrup and cream together till a little dropped in cold water forms a soft ball. Cool and beat till creamy; add the nuts and drop the mixture by spoonfuls on greased paper or plates.

January Thaw

2 cups brown sugar.   1 cup nuts.
½ cup milk.   Butter size of a walnut.

Put sugar and milk in a saucepan and let it dissolve slowly; add butter and let boil until it forms a ball when dropped into cold water. Remove from stove, add the chopped nuts and beat well. Turn into a buttered pan and, when cool, cut in squares.

Sea Foam

2 cups brown sugar.   1 teaspoon vanilla extract.
¼ cup water.   ½ cup chopped nuts.
1 egg white.

Boil the sugar and water together till a little dropped in cold water forms a soft ball. Pour the hot mixture over the stiffly-beaten white of the egg, beating while pouring. Add nuts and extract and beat vigorously till the candy stiffens. When nearly set drop by spoonfuls on paper. When cold the Sea Foam will harden so that it can be easily taken from the paper.

MEMORANDA

MEMORANDA

BEVERAGES

Tea

Use 2 teaspoons tea to a pint of water.

Have the water freshly boiling, scald the teapot, put in the tea, and pour on boiling water in the proportion given. Cover, and keep in a warm place, but where the tea will not boil, for three to five minutes to "draw." If it can not be used at once pour off the tea and discard the leaves. An earthen teapot is preferable.

Iced Tea

Iced tea is made the same as the hot beverage and may be prepared some hours before using, the infusion being poured off the leaves as soon as the strength is extracted, then cooled, and placed near the ice till required for use; or the tea may be made at the time of serving and chilled by the plentiful addition of cracked ice. The former is the most economical method. Iced tea should be taken clear and weaker than when served hot, and slices of lemon should be passed with it.

Boiled Coffee

2 tablespoons coffee to 3 cups water.
White of egg.

Grind the coffee moderately fine, add half the white of an egg to it and put into a perfectly clean coffee-pot. Add enough cold water to moisten the coffee, then pour the measured water over, cover the pot closely and boil ten minutes. Then pour in half a cup of cold water, draw the pot to the side of the range and allow it to stand five minutes to settle before serving. Never let the coffee boil after the cold water has been added.

Filtered Coffee

1 tablespoon of coffee to each cup.

Have the coffee finely ground, the coffee-pot hot and the water freshly boiling. Put the coffee into the strainer or upper part of the pot, measure the water and pour it slowly over the coffee. When it has filtered through, pour it again over the grounds, keeping the pot where the water will remain at the boiling point but not actually boil during the process. The pot may stand in a vessel of boiling water during the filtering process if desired.

Black or After-dinner Coffee

Make according to rule for Filtered Coffee, using twice the quantity of coffee to each cup of water. Serve in very small cups.

Café au lait

1 tablespoon of coffee to each cup.

Grind the coffee finely, and prepare as in Filtered Coffee, using only half the quantity of water. When filtered twice, pour off the coffee and add an equal amount of freshly scalded milk.

Iced Coffee in Perfection

1 pint good cold coffee.	1 pint milk.
½ teaspoon ground cinnamon.	Whipped cream.
	Cracked ice.

Have both coffee and milk thoroughly chilled; mix well, add cracked ice and, when serving, put the whipped cream on top of each glass and dust over with cinnamon.

Chocolate

2 squares chocolate.	Whipped cream.
2 teaspoons sugar.	4 tablespoons cold water.
3 cups milk.	1 teaspoon vanilla extract if liked.

Put the chocolate into a saucepan or the inner vessel of a double boiler with the water and sugar; cook over a gentle heat till the chocolate is melted, add the milk gradually and bring to the boiling point. Beat till foamy, flavor with vanilla, if liked, and serve with a spoonful of whipped cream on top of each cup.

Cocoa

2 tablespoons cocoa.	1 pint boiling water.
2 tablespoons sugar.	2 cups boiling milk.

Put cocoa and sugar in a saucepan, add to them half a cup of boiling water, and cook, stirring constantly, for five minutes. Add the remainder of the water, also the milk, and cook five minutes longer. Serve with cream if desired.

Chocolate Cream Nectar

2 squares (ounces) of chocolate.	3 cups water.
½ cup liquid coffee.	1 cup sugar.
	Whipped cream.
1 teaspoon vanilla extract.	

Melt the chocolate in a dry saucepan over a gentle heat, add the coffee (liquid) to it and cook two minutes, stirring constantly. Add sugar and water and cook five minutes. Chill, add vanilla and pour into glasses, each containing a tablespoon of whipped cream. Be sure the beverage is thoroughly chilled before serving.

Fruit Punch

2 pounds sugar.	Juice of 6 oranges and 4 lemons.
2 quarts water.	
2 quarts Apollinaris or other mineral water.	2 cups sliced strawberries.
	3 sliced bananas.
1 large pineapple, shredded.	1 cup raspberry or other fruit syrup.
Crushed ice.	

Boil the sugar and water together to form a syrup, add the Apollinaris, fruit and ice, with more water if the punch is too strong. Serve very cold.

Tea Punch

1 cup strong tea.	½ cup maraschino cordial.
1 sliced lemon.	1 cup sugar.
1 cup stoned cherries.	1 cup slightly crushed rasp-
1 quart water or carbon-	berries or strawberries.
ated water.	Cracked ice.

Pour the tea (hot) over the sugar, then when cold add the fruit, water, cordial and ice. Chill thoroughly before serving.

Blackberry Cordial

1 quart blackberry juice.	2 teaspoons each grated nut-
1 pound sugar.	meg, cinnamon and all-
1 teaspoon grated cloves.	spice.
1 pint brandy.	

Crush enough blackberries to give a quart of juice, put in a porcelain saucepan with the sugar, and the spices tied up in a bag. Cook fifteen minutes after it boils, skim, and cover closely till cold. Strain, add the brandy, and bottle and seal. This will keep for years.

Grape Juice

Grapes.   Sugar.

Pick grapes from the stalks, crush them and place over a slow fire till the juice runs freely; then strain through a fine cloth or jelly bag, pressing out all the juice. Measure, and to each quart use a cup and a half of sugar. Scald the juice, add the sugar, boil five minutes after all the sugar is melted, and bottle and seal closely.

Raspberry Vinegar

4 quarts raspberries.   2 quarts cider vinegar.
Sugar.

Crush two quarts of raspberries and pour the vinegar over them. Let stand two days, strain, and pour the same vinegar over the remaining two quarts of berries. Let stand again for two days and after straining, measure the liquid. Add for each pint one pound of sugar. Boil five minutes, skim, bottle and seal. Use two tablespoons to a tumbler of water.

Ginger Cup

4 oranges.	1 dozen cloves.
3 lemons.	½ teaspoon cinnamon.
24 lumps of sugar.	⅓ grated nutmeg.
1 cup shredded pineapple.	1 pint water.
1 quart ginger ale.	Cracked ice.

Push the cloves into the oranges and let them stand an hour that the flavor may be extracted. Rub the sugar over the rind of the oranges and lemons, then add juice of these to the sugar. Add the spices and pineapple and let stand two hours. At the time of serving put in the water and ginger ale and pour over the cracked ice.

Mint Cordial

1 large bunch of mint.	1 pint water.
Juice of 2 lemons.	Juice of 1 orange.
1 pound sugar.	1 cup pineapple juice.

Pick the leaves from the stalks of the mint, crush the leaves thoroughly, add the lemon juice and stand aside for one hour. Boil the water and sugar to a syrup, pour this over the lemon and mint; cool and strain. When cold, add the orange and pineapple juice and serve in glasses with a sprig of fresh mint in each.

Lime Punch

8 cubes sugar.	1½ cups water.
Juice of 2 oranges.	Cracked ice.
Juice of 2 limes.	Slice of pineapple.
2 crystallized cherries.	

Rub the cubes of sugar over the rind of the oranges and limes; then put the sugar in a bowl and pour the lime and orange juices over it. Add the water, and serve when the sugar is melted, chilling with plenty of cracked ice. Put in the pineapple and cherries at the moment of serving.

Claret Punch

⅔ cup sugar.
1 pint claret.
Juice of 2 lemons.
Cracked ice.
1 quart water.

2 sprigs mint.
1 sliced orange.
A few fresh strawberries if
   in season.

Dissolve the sugar in the water, add claret, lemon juice, ice and mint, crushing the latter slightly to extract its fragrance. Slice the orange thinly and add with the strawberries at the time of serving.

Mulled Cider

1 quart cider.
½ teaspoon whole allspice.

2 inches stick cinnamon.
3 eggs, well beaten.

Boil together the cider and spices for three minutes; add carefully to the well-beaten eggs, beating while adding. Strain, and serve very hot.

MEMORANDA

MEMORANDA

RECIPES FOR THE SICK

THE food eaten by a sick person has in many cases as much to do with rapid recovery as have drugs. It must be remembered that the palate is more sensitive in sickness than in health, both to seasonings and temperatures, so that less seasoning and more moderate degrees of heat and cold must be observed.

Daintiness in serving greatly influences the appetite of the patient, and, therefore, for this reason it is preferable to serve small portions and present the meal by courses rather than place all on the tray at one time. Have all hot beverages brought to the door of the sick room in a covered pitcher, then poured into the cup, thus avoiding the danger of spilling liquids into the saucer while carrying them to the patient.

Food should not be kept in the sick room between meals. It will be fresher and more appetizing if brought direct from storeroom or refrigerator when wanted.

When liquid foods are given, other receptacles than those for medicine should be used, as the association of the two is oftentimes unpleasant. When the dietary is limited, serve the foods that are permitted, in as many forms as possible to avoid sameness. For instance, beef tea may be given hot in the form of beef essence—as savory jelly, frozen, and as beef tea custard; practically the same food but more palatable because served in different forms.

Be very careful to keep such foods as milk, beef tea, etc., covered while in the refrigerator, to avoid contact with other or more odorous foods. If the refrigerator has more than one compartment reserve one exclusively for the use of the sick room.

Lemonade

1 lemon.   ½ pint cold water.
                    2 or 3 lumps of sugar.

Rub the sugar over the rind of the lemon to extract a little of the flavor. Squeeze the lemon juice over the sugar, add the water and stir till the sugar is dissolved. If the lemon is very large a little more water may be used. A thin slice of the lemon may be cut off before squeezing and placed in the glass with the lemonade.

A good substitute for the lemon juice is Horsford's Acid Phosphate.

Barley Water

1½ tablespoons pearl   ⅓ teaspoon salt.
    barley.   Juice of half a lemon.
1 quart cold water.   Also a little sugar if desired.

Wash the barley, pour the water over it and soak for several hours. Add salt and cook in a double boiler for at least three hours. Strain through cheese cloth or a fine strainer, flavor with the lemon, and add sugar if liked.

Toast Water

2 slices of stale bread   1 cup boiling water.
    toasted.   ⅙ teaspoon salt.

Toast the bread till golden brown and dry all through, or dry it in a moderately hot oven till golden brown and crisp. Pour the boiling water over it and add the salt; cover and set aside till cool Strain, and serve hot or cold. Some add milk, cream and sugar, and serve hot in place of tea or coffee.

Eggnog

1 egg.   1 tablespoon sugar.
⅔ cup milk.   1 tablespoon rum or brandy.
                    Pinch of salt.

Separate the white from the yolk of the egg, beat the latter and add sugar, salt and milk. Stir in the rum or brandy and beat, and add the white of stiffly-beaten egg at the last moment before serving.

Junket Eggnog

1 egg.	2 teaspoons sugar.
1 cup milk.	¼ junket tablet.
	2 teaspoons wine.

Separate the white from the yolk of the egg; add the sugar and wine to the yolk, then blend with the white. Have the milk lukewarm, add the egg mixture to it and immediately stir in the junket dissolved in a teaspoon of cold water. Pour at once into small glasses and grate a little nutmeg or cinnamon over the top. As soon as set put on ice to chill.

Albumenized Milk

1 egg white.	¼ cup lime water.
	1 cup milk.

Mix all ingredients, place in a shaker or covered jar and shake well. Strain and serve at once, plain or sweetened as preferred.

To Sterilize Milk

Pour fresh milk into small bottles, filling them almost full. Put absorbent cotton in the necks instead of corks, and place the bottles in a saucepan containing sufficient cold water to almost fill the pan; bring nearly to boiling point and let the bottles remain in the water fifteen minutes. Then remove and cool.

Wine Whey

1 cup milk.	½ cup sherry or port wine.

Boil the milk, add the wine and remove from the fire at once. Let stand till the curd is separated from the whey, then strain through a fine cloth and serve as it is, or reheat.

Acid Phosphate Whey

1 cup hot milk.
2 teaspoons sugar.

1 teaspoon Horsford's Acid Phosphate.

Heat the milk in a small saucepan over hot water or in a double boiler; add the Acid Phosphate and cook, without stirring, until the whey separates. Strain through cheese cloth and add the sugar. If more acid is desired, add two or three drops of Horsford's Acid Phosphate. Serve hot or cold.

Beef and Sago Broth

½ pound round steak or shin of beef.
1 pint water.

2 teaspoons sago.
1 egg yolk.
Salt.

Cut the beef into small pieces, add the water and let stand for half an hour; then cook in a double boiler two hours; strain, and press as much as possible of the meat pulp through a sieve. Add the sago, return to the saucepan and cook half an hour longer. Season and pour the broth over the yolk of the egg which has been lightly beaten. Serve at once.

Invalid's Tea

1 teaspoon tea.
1 cup scalded milk.
Sugar to taste.

Bring the milk quickly to the scalding point and pour it over the tea. Let the two infuse four minutes, strain, and serve with or without sugar. Tea made by this method nourishes as well as stimulates.

Clam Broth

6 clams in shells.
1½ cups water.

½ teaspoon butter, if allowed.

Scrub the shells and put them in a saucepan with one cup of water. Cook till the shells open, remove the clams, chop and return them to the saucepan with the water. Cook ten minutes, strain, and add the remaining water if necessary to reduce the strength of the broth. Season and serve.

Beef Juice

½ pound top round of beef.   Pinch of salt.

Broil the meat for about two minutes to "start" the juice, then press all the liquid from it with a meat press or an old-fashioned wooden lemon squeezer. Turn into a warm cup, or colored glass to disguise the color; add salt to taste, and serve. As this will not keep it must be prepared fresh for each serving.

Beef Tea

¼ pound round steak.   ½ pint water.
⅓ teaspoon salt.

Cut the meat in small pieces, the smaller it is cut the more easily it will give off its juices, or scrape it from the fibre. Add the cold water and stand aside for half an hour. Then place in a Mason jar, cover and stand in a saucepan of cold water; let it heat slowly to about 140 degrees and cook two hours; strain and season. It is better to have the jar raised from the bottom of the saucepan, that it may not come in too close contact with the heat of the range. Beef tea may be served hot, frozen, or in the form of a jelly, the latter consistency being obtained by the addition of one scant teaspoon of granulated gelatine soaked five minutes in a tablespoon of cold water and added to the beef tea as soon as the latter is strained. Stand in a cool place until set.

Oatmeal Gruel

1 cup water or milk.   1 tablespoon oatmeal or
¼ teaspoon salt.   rolled oats.

Have the water or milk actively boiling, shake the oats into it and cook fifteen minutes. Then place over hot water (a double boiler is best) and cook one hour. If the gruel is made with milk add the salt just before serving; with water, it may be put in earlier. Strain if desired to remove the particles of oats.

Corn Meal Gruel

1½ cups water.
1 slightly rounding table-
    spoon corn meal.

⅓ teaspoon salt.

Have the water salted and actively boiling, shake the meal gently into it and cook twenty minutes, stirring constantly; then turn the whole into a double boiler and cook two hours. Strain if desired.

Arrowroot Gruel

1 level tablespoon arrow-
    root.
1 cup milk.
¼ teaspoon salt.

2 tablespoons brandy or
    wine.
A very little sugar if de-
    sired.

Mix the arrowroot smoothly with a little of the milk, heat the remainder and, when boiling, put in the arrowroot and cook gently for ten minutes; add salt and sugar and at the moment of serving, the brandy or wine. Arrowroot contains little nutriment, but is useful as a vehicle for the serving of stimulants.

Irish Moss

1 small handful Irish moss.
3 cups milk.
1 tablespoon sugar.

⅓ teaspoon vanilla or other
    flavoring.

Wash and pick over the moss carefully, add it to the milk in a saucepan, and simmer the two till the moss begins to dissolve. A double boiler is preferable as it prevents too rapid cooking. In about twenty minutes, if the moss is dissolving, strain through cheese cloth, add sugar and flavoring, and turn into wet moulds or cups to cool. Serve with cream and sugar.

Savory Custard

1 cup beef tea or good stock (chicken or beef).	2 eggs.
	⅙ teaspoon salt.
	Pepper.

Beat the eggs till light but not foamy; add salt, and pepper if not objected to. Have the beef tea or stock hot and pour it over the eggs. Strain into greased cups or small moulds, and cover each with greased paper. Stand the moulds in a vessel of hot water and cook gently, either in the oven or over the fire, till the custard is set. As soon as a knife blade inserted in the custard comes out clean (not milky looking) remove from the fire. Unmould and serve hot or cold. Do not let the water surrounding the moulds boil or the custard will be honeycombed and less digestible.

Puffed Egg

1 egg.	Pinch of salt.

Separate the yolk from the white of the egg and beat the latter to a stiff froth, adding the salt. Turn into a cup and place in a steamer or vessel containing enough water to come halfway up the sides of the cup. Steam three minutes and if at the end of that time it is puffy looking, drop the unbroken yolk into the centre of the white, replace the cover of the pan and cook till the yolk is nearly set. Serve in the cup in which it is cooked.

Custard Soufflé

2 teaspoons butter.	⅓ cup milk.
1 tablespoon flour.	1 egg.
1 tablespoon sugar.	

Melt the butter, add the flour and blend smoothly without browning. Pour in the milk and cook three

minutes after boiling point is reached. Separate the
white from the yolk of the egg and beat each. Pour
hot mixture (let it cool a little) over the yolk, put in
the sugar and fold in gently the stiffly-beaten white.
Turn into two greased cups and bake in a steady
oven till firm — about fifteen minutes. Serve at
once with or without sauce.

Egg Cream

2 eggs
2 tablespoons sugar.

Grated rind and juice of
half a lemon.

2 tablespoons water.

Separate the whites and yolks of the eggs, and
beat the yolks with the sugar till well blended; add
the lemon juice, rind and water, and cook in a double
boiler, stirring constantly till the mixture begins to
thicken. Add whites of eggs beaten till thick, and
cook till the mixture resembles thick cream. Cool,
and serve in small individual cups or glasses.

Dainty Pudding

Thin slices of stale bread
without crust.

Fresh, hot stewed fruit
sweetened to taste.

Custard or cream.

Cut the bread into pieces about three inches long
and an inch wide. Line a cup with the pieces fitted
closely together; fill with hot, deep-colored fruit, and
place more bread over the top. Place a plate over
the pudding, put a weight on the plate, and set aside
till cold. Turn out, and serve with cream or custard.

Tapioca Jelly

⅓ cup tapioca.
1½ cups water.
⅓ cup sugar.

Juice and grated rind of half
a lemon.
2 tablespoons sherry or 1 of
brandy.

Have the water at the boiling point in a double
boiler, shake in the tapioca gently and cook for one

hour; strain if desired clear, or the tapioca can be left in. Add the sugar, lemon juice and rind, and when cool, the wine or brandy.

Chicken Chartreuse

1 cup cold cooked chicken.	1 cup chicken stock, or half
Salt, pepper and a little	stock and half cream.
grated lemon rind.	2 level tablespoons granu-
1 egg.	lated gelatine.

Mince the chicken finely, pass through a sieve and season to taste. Soak the gelatine for ten minutes in the cold stock or stock and cream, then heat to boiling point and, when the gelatine is dissolved, strain it over the chicken. Add the yolk of the egg lightly beaten, then the white beaten to a stiff froth. When partly cooled turn into a mould and put aside till very cold and set. Unmould and cut in thin slices.

Sweetbreads à la Newburg

1 pair of sweetbreads.	2 egg yolks.
2 tablespoons butter.	2 tablespoons sherry.
1 cup thin cream.	Salt and pepper to taste.

Parboil the sweetbreads in slightly salted water, cut them in cubes and cool. Melt the butter, put in the cubes and cook gently for five minutes. Add the cream and simmer five minutes longer; then put in the well-beaten yolks of the eggs and cook till they thicken, being very careful that the sauce does not curdle. Season to taste, and add the wine just before serving. This may be served on toast.

Beef Cakes

¼ pound very lean round steak.	Salt and pepper. Toast.

Cut the meat into strips, remove every particle of fat, and scrape the pulp from the fibre of the meat.

Season lightly, remembering that the palate is more sensitive to seasonings in sickness than in health. Form into very small balls or cakes, and broil about two minutes. Serve on rounds of buttered or dry toast.

Scraped Beef Sandwiches

¼ pound very lean steak.   Plain or buttered bread or
Salt and pepper.   toast.

Remove all fat, cut the meat into strips, scrape the pulp from the fibre, and season. Spread on thin slices of bread or toast, buttered or plain; cover with another slice, and cut into small strips.

MEMORANDA

palate i
an in i
d brou
tered a

d brea

ips, a
id or
over i

MEMORANDA

CARVING

THREE things are essential to good carving: first, a knowledge of the anatomy of the fish, fowl or joint to be served; second, a sharp carving knife; and, third, an acquaintance with the choice portions of the particular dish which is to be served.

FISH

In serving fish be careful not to break the flakes. With such fish as haddock, cod, flounder, etc., run the knife down the full length of the back fin to separate the flesh from the bone. Portions can be then divided easily.

With salmon be sure to serve a little of the thick and a little of the thin flesh to each person. The middle of a fish is usually the choicest in flavor, the tail part the most insipid.

When such fish as flounder or sole are fried it is wiser to fillet them — that is, remove the bone — before frying, as they are easier to serve when so prepared.

MEATS

Such joints as require it, from their lack of compact form, should be either tied, skewered or sewed into shape before cooking. When tying use white string; when skewering use steel skewers in preference to wooden ones, and when sewing use a trussing needle threaded with fine white string. Either method of securing the meat may be employed by the cook.

Serve gravy in a separate vessel from the meat, that the carver may work more easily.

Rib Roast. When the bone is left in, cut the meat in long, thin slices from the thin to the thick end of the meat. The thick, round muscle is the

233

choice portion of the roast, the meat at the thin end being more or less tough as well as containing an excessive proportion of fat. It is wiser to remove the greater part of this thin end and cook it in some other form than roast, where it can be used to greater advantage.

When the bone has been removed from a rib roast and the meat tied, skewered or sewed into shape, thin slices are to be cut across the upper surface of the meat. The skewers or tie threads must be left in place till the meat is cold so that it will retain its shape.

Sirloin or Porterhouse Steak. First insert the knife close to the bone and cut the meat away from it. Serve to each person a portion of the tenderloin and a portion of the meat from the upper side of the bone.

Round Steak. Cut in thin strips across the grain of the meat. This rule of cutting across the grain, instead of with it, holds good in the carving of all joints, whether roasts, pot-roasts, corned beef, beef à la mode or fresh boiled beef.

Fresh or Salt Ham. Cut in very thin, rather slanting slices, beginning near the narrow end of the joint. In this way fat and lean are more evenly distributed.

Tongue. If rolled, cut off the top slice and set it aside; then cut thin, even slices across the meat. If the tongue is not rolled, cut slices from the thicker portion of the meat, discarding the tip as this is dry and can be used to good advantage for potting or for sandwiches.

Leg of Lamb or Mutton. Have the fleshy side of the meat uppermost, and cut even slices down to the bone, beginning the carving about the middle of the leg and cutting towards the thick end of the joint. If the leg has been cut large, so that there are some of the chops with it (at the thick end) see that these are well cracked through the bones before cooking.

The chops are better served while the roast is hot, as the meat is drier when cold than the more fleshy part in the middle of the joint.

Loin of Lamb or Pork. Be very sure that the joints are well cracked, otherwise the meat can not be served neatly. Cut from the thin to the thick edge, having one rib bone in each slice of meat.

Crown Roast of Lamb is carved in the same manner as the loin, one bone to a slice, cutting from top to bottom of the meat.

POULTRY

Roast Fowl. First remove the leg, then the wing, and next the side bones. Cut thin slices from the breast, running from the head toward the tail. Cut off the wishbone and make a crosswise incision in the body of the bird for the removal of the dressing if this is used. If the tendons have been removed from the leg before cooking, this portion should be as tender as any other. Unless this has been done it is better to leave these joints to be made tender by further cooking.

Boiled Fowl is carved in the same manner, except that the breast is usually cut in thicker slices, and no dressing is served.

Broiled Chicken. Split down the back before cooking, and at serving time cut lengthwise through the breastbone, then, if large, into quarters, cutting across the breastbone. If the chicken is small, serve half to each person.

Duck and Goose. These are carved in almost the same manner as fowl; the breast, however, is not so thick, and the leg and wing joints lie somewhat closer to the body. The breast and wings of these birds are the choicest portions, the legs being generally reserved and deviled, or reheated in some other way. It is generally considered that the leg of a flying bird and the wing of a swimmer are, with the breast, the choicest portions.

TO BONE A FOWL

Wash and singe the bird, but do not draw it. Take a very sharp pointed knife and cut through skin and flesh the whole length of the back; then cut the flesh away from the bones, beginning at the neck, scraping all the meat from each bone as the work proceeds. On reaching the wings, cut them off close to the body, and after the meat is all cut from the carcass of the bird, the leg and wing bones can be more easily removed. These joints can be practically turned inside out, thus making the shape of the bird more symmetrical for stuffing and cooking. In boning, great precaution should be taken against breaking the skin, especially that of the breast. After boning, birds are stuffed with a savory dressing, the flesh sewed or tied in place over the stuffing, and either roasted or braised.

MEMORANDA

MEMORANDA

Rumford Chemical Works

Domestic

THE RUMFORD COMPANY,
    99 and 101 Commercial St., Boston, Mass.

THE RUMFORD COMPANY,
    407 Continental Building, Baltimore, Md.

THE RUMFORD COMPANY, 406 Rush St., Chicago, Ill.

H. M. ANTHONY CO.,
    261 and 263 Greenwich St., New York, N.Y.

LEFEBVRE-ARMISTEAD CO.,
    20–22 South 14th St., Richmond, Va.

MAILLIARD & SCHMIEDELL,
    N. E. cor. Sacramento and Front Sts.,
                  San Francisco, Cal.

Foreign

BOVRIL, Limited . . . . . London, E. C., England
GEORGES DETHAN . . . . Paris, France
NICOLA VALENTINO . . . . Naples, Italy
CHINA & JAPAN TRADING Co., Ltd., Yokohama, Japan
CHARLES MARKELL & Co. . . . . Sydney, N.S.W.
FELTON, GRIMWADE & Co. . . . Melbourne, Victoria
ELLIOTT BROS., Limited . . . Brisbane, Queensland
A. M. BICKFORD & SONS, Adelaide, South Australia
NEW ZEALAND DRUG CO. . . . . . New Zealand
CASSELS & Co. . Buenos Ayres, Argentine Republic
KING, FERRERIA & Co. . . . Rio de Janeiro, Brazil
J. MEYER . . . . Lima, Peru
DAUBE & Co. . . . . Valparaiso, Chili
HOLLISTER DRUG Co. . . . . . . Honolulu, H.I.
JOSÉ SARRÁ . . . . Havana, Cuba
JULIO LABADIE SUCRS Y CIA., City of Mexico, Mexico
HANS LUNDEN . . . . Christiania, Norway

Rumford Chemical Works

PROVIDENCE, R.I., U.S.A.

L. HORSFORD FARLOW, President.   N. D. ARNOLD, Treasurer.

Incorporated 1859   Cable Address "Rumford"

Organized especially for manufacture of the culinary phosphate preparations invented by the late Prof. E. N. Horsford, one of the founders of the company, who, at the time, occupied the chair in Harvard University endowed by the famous domestic economist, Count Rumford, and known as "the Rumford Professorship." From this relationship the title of the corporation was derived, this in turn giving the name Rumford to the thriving post-office village which has grown up about its principal manufacturing establishment, four miles from Providence on the New York, New Haven & Hartford Railroad.

Here are located the chemical factories with their interdependencies of repair shop, carpenter shop, machine shops, cooper shop, harness shop, one of the laboratories, etc., in fact all the necessary adjuncts that go to make up a great manufacturing enterprise of this kind. Here also has been established a library for the free use of the employees.

The main offices, packing department, printing and binding departments (producing labels, circulars, pamphlets, etc., used in the business), the principal and research laboratories, with other departments, occupy buildings owned by the company covering more than an entire square in the City of Providence, R.I.

HORSFORD'S ACID PHOSPHATE

(NON-ALCOHOLIC)

A solution of the phosphates of lime, magnesia, potash and iron in phosphoric acid. It is not a compounded patent medicine, but a scientific preparation recommended and prescribed by physicians of all schools.

INDIGESTION AND DYSPEPSIA. Half a teaspoonful Horsford's Acid Phosphate in half a glass of hot or cold water, or tea without milk, taken with each meal, or half an hour thereafter, makes the process of digestion natural and easy, and creates a good appetite.

NERVOUSNESS, EXHAUSTION, ETC. Horsford's Acid Phosphate supplies the waste of phosphates caused by every mental and physical exertion. It imparts new energy, increases the intellectual and physical power, and is an agreeable and beneficial food and tonic for the brain and nerves.

HEADACHE. Horsford's Acid Phosphate relieves headache caused by overwork, nervous disorders or impaired digestion.

TIRED BRAIN. Horsford's Acid Phosphate acts as a brain food, increasing the capacity for mental labor, relieving the tired brain, and imparting new energy to that organ.

WEAKENED ENERGY. Horsford's Acid Phosphate acts as a nutrient to the cerebral and nervous systems, giving vigor and renewed strength where there has been exhaustion.

SLEEPLESSNESS. Half a teaspoonful Horsford's Acid Phosphate in half a glass of water just before retiring brings refreshing sleep.

A DELICIOUS DRINK is made by adding a teaspoonful of Horsford's Acid Phosphate to a tumbler of water and sweetening to the taste.

FOR SALE BY DEALERS IN MEDICINES

If your druggist cannot supply you, we will mail you a trial size bottle upon receipt of 25 cents.

(241)